RUSSELL PETERS

CALL ME RUSSELL

with

Clayton Peters

and

Dannis Koromilas

ANCHOR CANADA

Anchor Canada edition published 2011

LIBRARY AND ARCHIVES CANADA CATALOGUING IN PUBLICATION

ISBN 978-0-385-66965-8

PRINTED AND BOUND IN THE USA

Published in Canada by Anchor Canada,
a division of Random House of Canada Limited

Visit Random House of Canada Limited's website: www.randomhouse.ca

10 9 8 7 6 5 4 3 2 1

TO CRYSTIANNA MARIE PETERS

"Help your brother's boat across, and your own will reach the shore."

—HINDU PROVERB

I'm Russell Peters' big brother. That's who I am now. Russell used to be Clayton Peters' little brother, but that all changed years ago when he decided to become a stand-up comic. When we were kids, if you had asked me if I'd be writing this today, I would have said that you were crazy. Neither Russell nor I ever expected to be where we are now. I won't deny that we both dreamed of it, but let's face it—these aren't the kind of dreams you share with people.

If I had told people that one day my baby brother would play a total of four sold-out shows at the Air Canada Centre or sell out Madison Square Garden, they would have just looked at me blankly, as if I'd said that I was going to be the first man on Mars. Despite our parents' modest aspirations for my brother—getting a union job at the Chrysler plant, or maybe becoming a civil servant—he had the nerve to reach beyond that.

We were latchkey kids, and my job was to make sure that my brother made it home from school safely and had something to eat. We'd walk in the front door and he'd be back outside in a flash to play with all his friends on the street. Even then, everyone was his new best friend. He was a happy and outgoing child and liked being the centre of attention. I was the opposite—reserved, cautious and quiet.

Almost forty years later, nothing has changed. His outgoing, charismatic personality has allowed him to get to where he is today. And my reserved, cautious and quiet nature has allowed me to be there, right behind him, making sure he's safe and secure as his fame and success continue to grow.

This book is not just about my brother, but about our family. My brother's act is primarily about race and culture, and so this book delves into the history of our own race and unique culture. My brother's journey to becoming one of the biggest stand-up comedians in the world began generations ago in Burhanpur, India, with our restless grandfather James Peters. It continued with our father, Eric, after he met our mother, Maureen, in Calcutta. Ultimately, the journey went on to include my brother and me growing up in a townhouse in Brampton, Ontario.

Within this book, my brother has been completely candid about everything from having ADD, to being bullied as a kid, to selling drugs, to his own tragic history with murders. He offers an up-close-and-personal, behind-the-scenes look at his life in comedy and his adventures in Hollywood and beyond.

When we started working on this book, we had discussed with the publishers the idea of creating a collection of my brother's humorous stories and new "bits"—essentially, a "funny book." After we started getting into it, we realized that we were delivering an honest, frank account of the son of immigrants who, for all of his success, is forever connected to his humble beginnings.

The stories and themes of this book are universal and can serve as a guidebook to all those kids whose parents discourage them from pursuing a life in show business. It proves that success can be achieved if you stick with something and if you're passionate about it. My brother has remained true to himself and followed his own path. In the late '90s, many people—including me—were telling him that he needed to go to Los Angeles in order to move his career forward. He said it wasn't time yet, that L.A. would call for him when it was ready. He was right. He waited patiently for the right moment, and that moment came after he exploded on YouTube in 2005.

The rest is history—or actually, his story . . .

—*Clayton Peters*

PART ONE

FAMILY

MATTERS

WHITE PEOPLE—
PLEASE BEAT YOUR KIDS. . . .
I'LL TELL YOU WHY

When I was growing up, I hung out with mostly black kids, but every now and then, some white kid would come and hang out with us, and we'd be like, "Wow! A white kid! I've heard so much about you!" But the problem was that when a white kid would show up, we'd all want to be like the white kid, and eventually, we'd start taking the white kid's advice on how to deal with our parents.

I remember hanging out with this little white boy, Ryan, when I was ten years old. I went to his house after school one day. His parents never beat him and they never even yelled at him. He could do anything he wanted and nothing was going to happen to him. We walked into his house after school one day and his mom says, "Ryan, go clean your room."

Ryan says, "FUCK YOU, BITCH!"

I go, "Ryan, you can't talk to your mom like that!"

"Yes I can. She's a JACKASS."

"Don't say that, man. She'll hit you."

Then Ryan says, "No she won't. She not allowed to."

I'm like, "What are you talking about? My parents hit me."

"Well the next time they try that, you tell them to fuck off."

"Are you sure?"

"Trust me. It works for me."

So I went home . . . for the last time. I walked into the house and Dad goes, "Russell, come and do the dishes."

"Fuck you, Dad!"

Dad says, "What the hell did you say to me?! Do I look like Ryan's mom? SOMEBODY gonna get a-hurt real bad."

That was dad's threat right before he beat me. I hated that threat. You know why? Because he'd always say *somebody*. He'd never tell you it was *you*. You knew it was you, but he'd give you this hope that it wasn't. In the back of my head, I'm thinking, "Please please let it be my brother."

When I saw that little brat Ryan a few days later at school, I was like, "Hey, your little plan the other day almost got me killed."

"Ah, sorry, dude. I forgot to tell you the other part. If your dad's still going to hit you, threaten to call Children's Aid."

I ask, "Why?"

"Because if you phone Children's Aid, your dad's going to get in trouble. You don't even have to call, just pretend. It will scare the crap out of him."

So I'm ten years old, and someone's telling me I can scare the crap out of my dad. That's like finding kryptonite. I thought I'd try it.

The next time I was about to take a beating, I stopped my dad and said, "DON'T DO IT! I'll phone Children's Aid." Ever had your parents call your bluff?

"You'll do what?" Dad says.

"I'll phone Children's Aid."

"Is that right. . . . Well, let me get you the phone, tough guy."

"Dad, what are you doing? If I phone Children's Aid, you'll get in trouble."

"I might get in a little bit of trouble, but I know that it's going to take them twenty-two minutes to get here. In that time, SOMEBODY gonna get a-hurt real bad!"

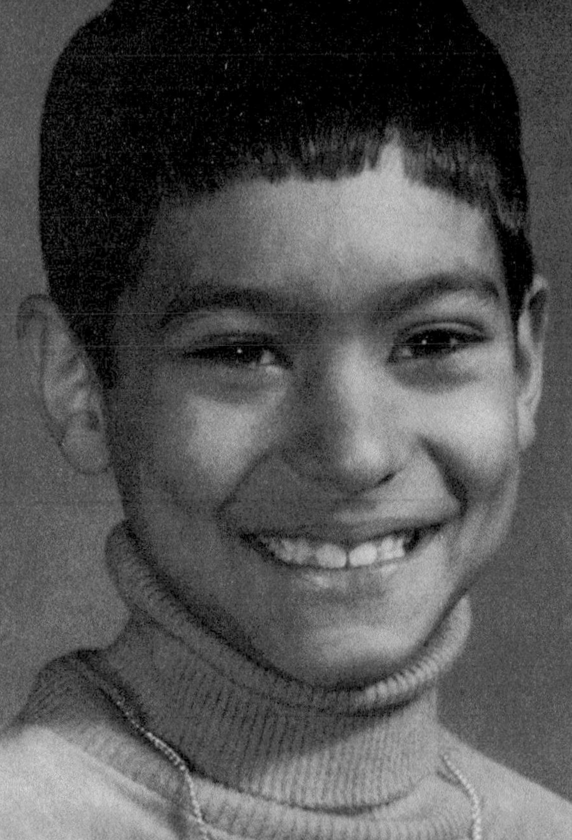

CHAPTER 1

CALL ME RUSSELL

I'M NEVER just a comic. No matter how people describe me, there's always something before my name or my profession. There's always that hyphen: South-Asian comic, Indo-Canadian comic, South-Asian-Canadian comic, Canadian-born-Indian comic, Brampton-raised stand-up comic. Obviously, I'm not the first stand-up comic in the world, but I know that I'm the first stand-up who looks like me, and the first to have done some of the things I've done. I guess that's what happens when you're the first at something . . . people think it needs to be qualified by something else. To my friends and family, though, there's no hyphen. They just call me Russell.

To me, I'm just a comedian who happens to be Indian . . . or wait, Canadian . . . or Indo-Canadian . . . Anglo-Indian, South-Asian, South-Asian-Canadian? Jeez, even I'm confused.

Both of my parents are Anglo-Indian. Both of their parents were Anglo-Indian, and before that one of their great-grandfathers or great-great-grandfathers was British, Welsh, Scottish or Irish—one of those *ish*es. That's what it is to be an Anglo-Indian. Somewhere in your genes is a British father and an Indian mother. Anglo-Indians, or AI's, mixed with the British when they occupied India. That's why my name is Russell Peters instead of something you'd be more likely to expect for a guy who looks like me, both of whose parents were born in India. Anglo-Indians come in all shades—from blond-haired and blue-eyed to dark-skinned with very traditional "Indian" features.

To my friends and family, there's no hyphen. They just call me Russell.

Anglo-Indians are a very small, unique community as well as a dying one, a remnant from the Raj. My cousins have surnames like Brown, Page, Waike and Matthias and first names like Mikey, Gordon, Bruce, Andrew, Patty, Tina, Ann, Claire, Stephen, Tanya, Marissa, Darren, Charlene . . . I still get some flak from older Anglo-Indians because I usually just say I'm Indian instead of specifying that I'm *Anglo*-Indian. That's a bit of a thing for AI's—you've got to be specific about saying that you're one of them. They don't necessarily see themselves as Indian, nor do they see themselves as English, just as the Indians don't see them as Indian and the English don't see them as English. The way I see it, once you cross the ocean, nobody cares what subset or group you come from. Once you're here, you're just another Indian—whether you like it or not. It's kind of like when Indians go on about being from a specific caste. Really, who gives a shit? Is an AI really going to get treated any better in Canada, the States or England because he's a Brahmin? That's the beauty of these countries: Canadians don't care about that kind of caste crap—we're all just brown to them.

Back in the mid-eighteenth century, the British realized that it was going to be impossible to rule more than 120 million Indians with just forty thousand or so Brits, so they came up with a program to intermarry with the locals to strengthen their hold on the country. It was always a British male with an Indian female—anything else would have been scandalous. *And*, as my dad always liked to point out, the children of an Indian male and British female were called Eurasian and not Anglo-Indian. Ben Kingsley is Eurasian, since his father's Indian and his mom is English. See? Anglo-Indian, Eurasian—they're not the same thing.

English is the first language for Anglo-Indians, even in India. Hindi was only spoken to the servants or co-workers—or when my parents didn't want me to know what they were saying. My grandmother's Hindi was so bad that her boss asked her to please not speak it. AI's are Christian by religion—either Anglican or Catholic, for the most part. We don't consider ourselves converts. Obviously, at some point we were converted, but that was generations ago through intermarriage, and it will be through intermarriage that the very small community of AI's will eventually become extinct. I don't say this in a negative way. It's not as if I'm asking for a telethon to save the Anglo-Indians, it's just a statement of fact.

While the British were in India, the Anglo-Indians were sort of middle managers. They spoke like the British and looked like the Indians. They could communicate with the locals and behave like the foreigners. They enjoyed good jobs in the railways, customs, post and telegraph, and as teachers. Some even ended up as entertainers—as bandleaders, singers and actors. Engelbert Humperdinck, Cliff Richard and Merle Oberon ('30s movie star) are noted AI's, although I don't think they publicize it that much.

When the British left India in 1947, Anglo-Indians were at loose ends. Job opportunities, especially for the men, were difficult to get and the Anglo-Indians began leaving India—coming to Australia, England, Canada and even some to the States.

One of the most commonly asked questions I get is "What's your *real* name?" Thing is, I usually get this question from Indians, not from white people. What can I say? If you don't get my name, you'll need to check in with my brother, Clayton, or my mom and dad, Maureen and Eric.

Speaking of Mom and Dad, I guess that's where my story really starts. My dad, Eric Peters, was born in Bombay in 1925. Dad's mom died a few months after he was born, from complications connected to his birth. His father, James Peters, had moved to Bombay from Madras and worked as a telegraph operator for the railways. My grandfather hated the big city; he found it too dirty and crowded. In 1935, he packed up my dad, Dad's older brother, Arthur, and their ten-day-old baby sister, Eileen, as well as my grandfather's new wife, Blossom, and moved to the small village of Burhanpur in the middle of India. (Burhanpur is where Mumtaz Mahal, the third and most beloved wife of the Mughal emperor Shah Jahan I, died and remained

My grandfather, James Peters.

until Shah Jahan had completed the Taj Mahal as her mausoleum.) Since my grandfather worked for the railways, he could basically transfer wherever he wanted—as long as it was on a rail route.

James Peters (left), my father (right) and my cousin James as a child.

My grandfather bought twenty acres of land in the countryside, about a kilometre from the train station and outside of the village of Burhanpur. He built a large, open bungalow surrounded by lemon and mango trees. He became a gentleman farmer who grew peanuts, cotton and wheat. He acquired two horses, a couple of bulls, goats and buffaloes. He also kept a number of greyhounds, whippets and German shepherds. The dogs came in handy for the family's frequent hunting excursions in the neighbouring hills.

To hear my dad tell it, his childhood in Burhanpur was the absolute best of times—hunting, camping, fishing, sleeping outdoors, surrounded by his boarding-school friends, cousins, siblings, and of course his dad, whom my father idolized. My grandfather was almost six feet tall, compared to my dad's five-foot-six or so. I guess that's where I get my height from—not that I'm that tall, but I am the tallest guy in my relatively short family.

After serving as a radio operator during the war, Dad eventually moved to Calcutta, but continued to go back and forth to his beloved Burhanpur. It was in Calcutta, at the age of thirty-nine, that Dad met Mom. Mom was a fair-skinned, ninety-three-pound beauty with thick black hair and a taste for the latest "western" dresses, most of them handmade by

The Anglo-Indian lifestyle in Calcutta. The very cool KK (middle, with sunglasses) and my grandmother Sheila (far right, with sunglasses and cigarette).

her seamstress grandmother. For Dad, it was love at first sight. He used to see my mom around town and decided that she was the one. Dad was a womanizer, sixteen years her senior. Dad would see Mom on a rickshaw and would follow right behind on his scooter, honking the horn to make the rickshaw man run faster. Mom would get fuming mad and was convinced that Dad was an ass.

One night, at their mutual friend Rene's flat, Dad decided that it was time to make his move. Rene made the introduction. Mom was unimpressed; however, they both lingered at the party long enough that it started to get dark, and too late for Mom to get back to her family's flat. Dad swooped in and offered her a ride home on the back of his scooter, and Mom accepted . . . reluctantly. What would her mother say when she arrived home riding on the back of a scooter with a much older man, a man who was only a year younger than her own mother?

It didn't take long for Mom to see that Dad was a bit of a show-off but not a complete jerk.

It didn't take long for Mom to see that Dad was a bit of a show-off but not a complete jerk, and when he started regularly taking her on the back of his scooter, the poor rickshaw man was out of a job. After a few more rides home, Mom eventually said to Dad, "I think you'd better come in and meet my mother." He had his foot in the door.

Dad walked into the one-bedroom flat on Ganesh-Chandra Avenue that housed my mom; her older brother Maurice and younger brother Roger; my grandmother's second husband, the very cool KK (more on him in a minute); my great-grandmother Jessie; and my striking grandmother Sheila. My grandmother sized him up, and when he left, she declared she was unimpressed by this scooter-man courting her daughter. First, he was too old, and second, he was Protestant. "It's not a good match," she warned Mom, adding, "He's a Freemason. They're devil worshippers." I'm not sure what happened next, but somehow, between Dad being a jerk and now a devil worshipper, Mom was smitten.

Let me tell you about my mom's stepfather, KK, whose real name was Kewal Kohli. He was a Punjabi Hindu who married my grandmother after she divorced my grandfather, Christopher Waike. We called him Dadda, but to everyone else he was just KK.

My grandfather Christopher had taken up with another woman when my mom was in her early teens, and my grandmother filed for divorce. KK took Christopher's place. He adored my grandmother and she adored him. He was the coolest guy I have ever met. Even as a small child, I could see that this guy was an operator. He knew how to work a room and could get things done. Running late for a flight? KK could get you right through the usual customs formalities and straight to the gate without any hassles. He was charismatic and charming. Being a Hindu never seemed to be any issue. I remember visiting him as a kid in 1975 and seeing this huge portrait of Sai Baba (a Hindu holy man) in their flat on Elliot Road. There was also this small altar with a statue of Jesus, Mary and other Catholic icons. I remember being a little creeped out by the altar. I don't know why, but there was just something scary about it.

But back when Dad was courting Mom, he was not KK's first choice of marriage partners for her. KK had hoped to make a match of his own for "his" daughter. Eventually, though, he too was won over by Dad and accepted him into the family.

So back to Mom being smitten . . . Once Dad realized he was making progress with this woman, he immediately went back to his father and told him, "Dad, I've met her, the girl of my dreams."

"You mean you've met the right girl *again*?"

Dad was a bit of a player, which explains why he wasn't married at the age of thirty-nine. Before he met Mom, he was having a great time in Calcutta and had developed something of a reputation as a playboy—like father, like son? Anyhow, this wasn't the first time he'd told his dad he'd met the woman of his dreams.

"This one is different. She's the one," Dad said.

Granddad asked, "How old is she?"

"Sixteen years younger than me."

"Good choice, son!"

Mom and Dad were married on December 28, 1963. One hundred and fifty people attended the wedding at St. Francis Xavier Church in the Bowbazar section of Calcutta. Mom kept Dad waiting half an hour at the church, while his friends took bets on whether she would show up. After the wedding, they took bets as to how long the marriage would last. According to Mom, people said it wouldn't last because of the age difference. According to Dad, people said it wouldn't last because he was Protestant and Mom was Catholic. The church sanctioned the marriage only on the basis that any children be raised Catholic. When Dad died in 2004, they had been married forty years.

Mom and Dad on their wedding day.

Mom and Dad got a small one-bedroom flat on Theatre Road, which they shared with Dad's pal, Trevor Lewis. Work opportunities were slim, and Dad knew that they and their still-unborn children would have better opportunities overseas. Dad wanted to go to England, where a lot of his pals had already moved and were doing well. Mom had no intention of setting foot on British soil and warned Dad that if he went to England, he'd be going alone. She hated grey and gloomy weather and had heard stories of how badly the Tommies—British soldiers in India—had once treated her beloved Grandmother Jessie when she had worked for the Women's Army Corps during the war. Every day, the WAC would be picked up by truck and taken to various locations around Calcutta. On one particular day, a Tommy thought he'd be smart and told the driver to accelerate just as Jessie was getting on. The truck lurched forward, and

Jessie landed on her face, chipping a tooth and scraping her skin. She pulled the laughing Tommy down from the truck and slapped him. My very tough great-grandmother made sure that she wouldn't be disrespected by the Tommies ever again. Mom had also seen the 1935 version of the film *David Copperfield* several times, and this too had put her off of England.

Now that England was off the table, my parents began to explore other options. Some Anglo-Indians were leaving for Australia, but it never occurred to Mom and Dad to move there. Of course, the United States was also an option; but my father, who was always very aware of social and political climates, felt that a darker, brown-skinned man stepping into that country in the mid-'60s would be asking for trouble. He knew what street riots looked like—having seen the Hindu–Muslim riots in India in 1947—and he was well aware of what was happening with the civil rights movement in the U.S. He knew what Martin Luther King and Malcolm X were doing. Having seen India go through its growing pains after independence, and self-conscious about his own skin colour, it didn't make a lot of sense to him to try to raise a family in the States.

Word began to spread among Anglo-Indians about another country that had opened its doors: Canada. It was a young country that needed an educated workforce to grow, and while many immigrants arriving there couldn't speak English, Mom and Dad were fluent. They should get in, no problem—right?

When my father was alive, he'd occasionally tell me stories of those early years, and I have to say that even though decades had passed since his arrival in Canada, his memories of those days never lost their edge. Even before Dad arrived in this country, he had to face the hard truth about what it would be like as a new immigrant in Canada. In his first encounter with a Canadian consular representative working in Calcutta, whose job it was to screen immigration candidates, my dad was told, matter-of-factly, "You'll never get a job in Canada, Mr. Peters. You're just too old." My father was thirty-nine, going on forty.

My dad was told, matter-of-factly, "You'll never get a job in Canada, Mr. Peters. You're just too old."

"That's okay, I'll be fine," my father replied.

Mr. Walker, the immigration officer, continued: "What Canada needs and wants is young people. They want people who speak English."

My dad stared dumbfounded and said, "And what the bloody hell am I speaking to you in? I'm speaking to you in English, aren't I?"

Mr. Walker didn't have a comeback. My father railed. "Now tell me, you have immigrants already in Canada who don't speak English, do you not? How come they're allowed in?"

"They're cheap labour. They're the construction workers, and they clean the streets." My dad shrugged his shoulders and asked, "So you're discriminating against me *because* I speak English?"

That was my dad's first encounter with a government official. Amazingly, my mom and dad were accepted into the country, under the condition that my mother, who was pregnant with my brother at the time, give birth to the child in India. My father's sister, Eileen, had also applied to emigrate and was accepted.

In 1965, less than a year after my big brother, Clayton, was born, my parents picked up and left, choosing Canada as the country in which they would raise my brother and later have me.

Eric and Maureen Peters landed in Toronto's west end in August 30, 1965. They had with them their savings—a grand total of $100—and two steamer trunks that contained all of their wedding gifts, Mom's best linen . . . and a tiger skin from Dad's last big hunt in India. For the first ten days in Canada, they stayed with friends, Uncle Mervin and Auntie Edna, while Dad worked odd jobs to put together enough money for a deposit on their first apartment in Canada, a one-bedroom on Rockcliffe Boulevard in Toronto.

Once that was taken care of, the next hurdle became furniture. They had nothing at all, so they went to Caplan's on Weston Road, a furniture store still there to this day. They had no money and decided to level with the salesman.

They said, "We're new immigrants. We have no money and we need to get some furniture."

The salesman asked, "Well, how's your credit rating?"

My mom and dad looked at each other in total confusion, then asked, "What's a credit rating?"

You see, India didn't have anything like that; a system where you could actually borrow against future earnings was beyond their wildest imaginings. To their "credit," the Caplan family who owned the store proved to be good and trusting people who enabled my parents to get credit until they got on their feet. My mom and dad brought furniture home soon after, and although it was nothing extravagant, it was a start.

My dad got a job soon after arriving. He went from working in Calcutta as a white-collar, trilingual (Dad spoke English, Hindi *and* German) public-relations person for a German engineering company called Koppers India Ltd. to a paint mixer for CIL in Rexdale. The transition crushed my dad—to the point where he hated the smell of paint until the day he died. There were days when he thought he'd thrown away everything he'd ever accomplished, only to start at the bottom. It was hell.

He hated his work and he hated Canada. He also became aware of the open racism towards him at the time. Here's the thing: my mom is very light-skinned, and when she arrived in Toronto, no one could tell where she was from. But my dad was dark, and even in India, within the Anglo-Indian community, he was very much aware of his colour. When walking down the street with Mom in Toronto, he noticed that people would look at them funny. In Dad's mind, they were asking themselves why a girl like that would marry a darkie like him. He was very sensitive to what he viewed as open racism in Canada.

And there were other questions, too, like "Where are you from?"

"I'm from India," Dad would say to whoever was asking.

"But if you're from India, then why do you speak such good English? Where did you learn?"

"On the plane ride over," Dad would answer sharply. He'd often use sarcasm, wit and his command of the English language to disarm the ignorant. Most strangers never saw him coming. They were expecting him to come at them with something lame, in a thick Indian accent and without any humour—but he was quick-witted and didn't suffer fools gladly. He'd never hesitate to throw out a quick barb or observation at someone—in the checkout line or just in passing—and was always amused by their blank expressions he got in return. He called it a "dah look" (not "duh" but "dah") and would imitate the person—mouth hanging open and a blank stare on his face. I should also point out that in my act, as much as I make my dad sound like he had an Indian accent, in fact he sounded more like a British army officer. Think Higgins from *Magnum P.I.* or Sir John Gielgud's Hobson, the butler in the movie *Arthur.* That was closer to Dad's voice and delivery in real life.

In my act, as much as I make my dad sound like he had an Indian accent, in fact he sounded more like a British army officer.

At home, in Mom and Dad's new, sparsely furnished Canadian apartment, Christmas was getting closer and closer. When Christmas Eve finally arrived, it consisted of Mom and Dad and my brother. No tree, no decorations, no turkey, no presents. Nothing. My dad walked home that night from his job at CIL, and on his way he stopped at the Kresge's department store on Dundas Street in the Junction, where in the bright window he saw a beautifully decorated little Christmas tree. It was ten minutes before closing time. He quickly entered the store, spotted an employee and politely asked to speak to the manager. When the manager arrived, Dad asked, "Can you sell me that tree in the window?"

"We can't, sir. We have to keep it there for Christmas." It was then that my father decided to tell the man his story, to explain that he was a new immigrant and he was going to his empty home and to his family on Christmas Eve with not a thing to bring them. I guess the guy felt sorry for him, because he gave my dad the tree—with all the ornaments, too. So a few minutes later, my dad was on the sidewalk outside of Kresge's, walking home, grinning, with a fully decorated Christmas tree under his arm. Once he brought the tree inside the house, he plugged in the lights, and the little family of three began their first Christmas in Canada.

Although both my parents were Anglo-Indian and Catholic, my mother had no idea what the traditional Canadian Christmas meal was supposed to be, so she made some rice and daal. Truth be told, this was actually all she could cook. She had never learned to cook back home because her family had a cook. Now, I know this may sound strange considering that she grew up in a small flat with six people, but having a cook or other servants wasn't something that was exclusive to the very wealthy in India at that time. With millions living below the poverty line, there was always someone you could hire to get things done, and it didn't cost much. Mom says that Dad never complained about rice and daal for dinner, or her still-undeveloped cooking skills. Soon she mastered mince curry, a dish that we'd all come to love, especially my dad.

On Christmas Day, Mom went out into the hallway to wish her neighbours a happy holiday.

"Merry Christmas to you, Maureen!" they said. "And where were you yesterday?"

"Where were we? We were home."

Her neighbours scolded her, saying, "Oh, you should have come over!"

My mom, a little shocked, replied, "How could we come over? You didn't invite us. Am I supposed to just knock on somebody's door and say here I am?" To which they replied, "Yes. That's how it's done here." One woman even said that her husband had won a huge turkey in a contest and they hadn't even gotten around to cooking it.

"Would you like it?" the woman said, dumping the turkey she didn't want on my mom. I wasn't even born yet, but somehow I can see this image of my bewildered mom, standing in the hallway of the apartment block on Christmas Day, holding a massive raw turkey in her arms.

"What do you want me to do with this?" Mom asked, as the woman turned on her heel and went back to her apartment.

"Cook it," was the response.

There was a Canadian lady across the street that my mother had started babysitting for, and she knocked on her door.

"Could you please tell me how to cook this turkey?" my mom pleaded. Eventually, the bird was cooked, and eaten, and my family's first Canadian Christmas was, if not successful, then at least over.

There were a lot of moments like this among my family's first experiences in Canada, and over the years my parents have recounted these stories to me and my brother many times. There's no anger, no resentment; they were just new immigrants adjusting to a strange and very, very different land.

My mom had a good sense of humour about some of these misadventures, but my dad was miserable in Canada at the beginning. He missed his father a lot, and his father was not well. He cried when he thought of home, and it really disturbed him to think of his dad in ailing health and being so far away. We have a thing about dads in my family. I've got it, Brother's got it, and Dad had it, too. We all idolize our fathers. We romanticize them and remember them as larger-than-life characters who had great adventures drinking, hunting, travelling. As much as we remember the mundane details of our day-to-day lives with Dad—seeing him leave for work at six in the morning, doing groceries, and always being somewhat angry because he had to get up at five-thirty in the morning—we focus more on who he was as a man, his sense of humour, his style and who he was before we were born.

In 1967, Dad followed his heart and went back home. He didn't have enough to pay for the flight, so he bought a fly-now-pay-later ticket on Air India. It was planned as only a ten-day trip, but my mom didn't believe that was really the extent of it. I think she believed he might never return. Dad begged Mom to go with him, but she refused.

"You brought us here to this new place," she said. "I've given everything up in India, and now I'm staying here, no matter what." That's my mom, strong-willed and determined, and one of the few people I have ever met with the power to shut my dad up instantly. My mother, always hopeful and encouraging, kept pressing him to stick it out. She kept reinforcing her belief in him, telling him to give himself a chance, a little more time at least to forge his way in this new place.

But Dad went to India on his own. Despite my mother's fears, he returned exactly ten days later. "I had to come back" was all he said. After living in Toronto for over a year, it had been a real shock for him to see India through new eyes. Despite the despair regarding his quality of life in Canada, he'd gotten used to the clean streets and orderly society that Canada offered. He could never go back and there was no looking back. Like it or not, Canada was home now.

Despite all the early difficulties my mom and dad encountered, I have never once caught my parents looking back on their lives and wishing they had never left India. With time, they became truly happy in Canada.

They moved from Rockcliffe Boulevard to sharing a two-story flat above a store on Bloor Street, near Christie. They shared the flat with Aunty Elsie and Uncle Jimmy and their four children, their grandmother, two older sisters and one of their husbands.

Mom got a job at the Garfield magazine kiosk at the Eglinton subway station—working for a dollar an hour. Dad left the various blue-collar jobs—working at CIL, as a night security guard at Mount Pleasant Cemetery, as a police dispatcher at Toronto's 51 Division—and eventually landed a clerical job at William Mercer in downtown

Toronto. Mom and Dad got another flat of their own on Avenue Road, and Mom started working in the cash office at Holt Renfrew.

My parents laid the groundwork for our success. They gave me and my brother all the things that they had never had themselves back home. And when it comes down to it, I think that's what so many immigrant parents hope for: not necessarily a great life for themselves—a *better* life, perhaps—but at least the promise of an easier one for their kids. I know my parents are thankful that they ended up in this country. They couldn't imagine living anywhere else. I firmly believe that I wouldn't be Russell Peters if they had emigrated to Australia,

I think that's what so many immigrant parents hope for: not necessarily a great life for themselves . . . but at least the promise of an easier one for their kids.

England or the States. I've become who I am not just because of who my parents were but because I was able to grow up in Canada—and not just in Canada, but in Toronto, and, of course, Brampton.

As I write this, I'm on the cusp of turning forty, the same age my dad was when he arrived in this country. It's humbling to think of him landing here with only a hundred dollars in his pocket versus where I am at the same age. All my stuff—and it is just stuff—the houses, the cars, the money . . . it all started with that hundred dollars in his pocket forty-five years ago.

CHAPTER 2

DAD WANTED A GIRL

A LITTLE-KNOWN FACT: I was supposed to be a girl. Yep. My dad wanted a Dominique, but he got a Russell instead. He had this thing about a perfect "million-dollar family"—a family with a boy and a girl. Now we *are* a million-dollar family, just not in the way Dad imagined back then.

I was born in Mount Sinai Hospital in Toronto on Tuesday, September 29, 1970. My parents and six-year-old brother were living on Indian Road in the west end of Toronto. Dad had purchased the house—the first home he and Mom ever owned—a year earlier. (I guess if you're from India and don't know where to buy, Indian Road is the obvious choice.)

After Brother, Mom and Dad tried for another baby. Mom had a miscarriage before having me, but I'm pretty sure that if that kid had survived, there would be no Russell Peters.

When I was still a bump in Mom's belly, Dad was willing me to be a girl. When it was time for me to disappoint him, I did it my way. Mom's water broke at the very convenient hour of four in the morning. My parents didn't want to wake up the neighbours, so they just put my brother in their bed and told him to stay put while Dad took Mom to the hospital. They called a cab, locked the door behind them and jumped in the taxi when it arrived. When the taxi driver realized the woman in the back was in labour, he started "having kittens"—Mom's polite way of saying he was shitting his pants. He was sure she was about to pop a baby in the back seat of his cab. To calm him down, Mom asked, "So what's your name?"

"George," the taxi driver said.

"Tell you what, George. If I have this baby in your cab, I'll name it after you."

Now the name George works for George Clooney, but I don't think I'd make a very good George, so I decided to hold off being born until George the cabbie was out of the picture.

At five-thirty, while Mom was in the labour room, Dad rushed home to look after my brother. At 10:14 in the morning, out I popped.

When Mom called Dad to tell him the news, Dad clammed up completely. He was totally crushed that I was a dude. He had his heart set on a girl, and, well, I'm really, really not one. The closest I get is when I take a really cold shower.

When Dad got to the hospital, he didn't even want to look at me.

When Dad got to the hospital, he didn't even want to look at me. Mom urged him to go to the nursery and see me for himself, and all he could say in response was "Give me time." He did go and check me out later, and according to Mom, I won him over.

Mom had asked one of her co-workers to be my godmother, and the woman agreed on the condition that Mom call me Russell, so it's a good thing I wasn't born in George's cab or there could have been a problem. My middle name, Dominic, is my grandmother's choice . . . kind of. A strict Catholic, she prayed to St. Dominic for my safe delivery and agreed to name me accordingly if all went well. Dominic was also the name of my Italian godmother's husband.

My mother claims I was a delightful baby, as most mothers do. She compared me to my brother, who would stay awake all night and sleep all day. He also wouldn't let her leave his sight. She says that I was the opposite—slept when I was supposed to, happy, cheerful. Who knew?

A rare photo of me as a child, bawling.

We moved from Indian Road to a two-bedroom basement apartment in a four-story building on Barrie Place in Waterloo when I was one. Dad decided to pursue his real love, journalism, and was studying at Conestoga College.

After about a year in Waterloo, we moved back to Toronto, to another one-bedroom basement apartment on Brock Avenue. The building is still there, but it's all boarded up now. It looks completely out of place on the street.

My own memory of my life kicks in around the age of four. I vividly remember the house we lived in on Norval Street in the west end of Toronto. It was like we were living two lives at the time: one during the week and another on the weekends. On weekdays, my brother and I would go to school and both Mom and Dad would work. I was in junior kindergarten and my brother was in Grade 4 at St. Cecilia's Catholic School on Evelyn Avenue—St. C's, as it was and is still called today. We'd take two TTC buses from Norval Street just to get there.

This was sort of the beginning of my brother taking care of me—he'd hold my hand to and from school and join me at lunchtime to make sure I ate my lunch. I had a little red lunch box shaped like a barn, with a milk container shaped like a silo that fit nicely inside. Lunch was a peanut-butter-and-jam sandwich or SPAM or a cheese sandwich. When my brother and I got home, he'd usually make a snack for us to eat—macaroni and cheese, toast, wieners and beans—and we'd wait until Mom and Dad got home.

Evenings were a mad rush of Mom ironing all our clothes, making our lunches and cooking dinner. She was now working in the accounting office at *The Globe and Mail* on Front Street. Dad was working as a federal meat inspector with the Department of Agriculture in the slaughterhouses along St. Clair Avenue between Keele Street and Runnymede Road. It was a steady union gig, but Dad would come home exhausted at the end of the day. He used to describe what it was like walking around in two inches of animal guts and sticking his hands inside carcasses for eight hours each day. When he got home, he'd have a nap, a pre-dinner drink and then dinner—by himself—at around nine-thirty or so. There wasn't a whole lot of time for anything else but preparation for the next day.

This was a far different life from the one my parents had in India, where at the end of the workday there was afternoon tea and often friends or family dropping by in the evening for drinks or potluck dinner. The cook would have dinner ready by seven or eight. Your clothes would be cleaned and pressed by the *dhobi*, and the flat would be cleaned by the sweeper. Your lunch for the next day would be made fresh in the morning and delivered in a tiffen-carrier by the cook or a tiffen service to your office. Meanwhile, as any immigrant will gripe, life in Canada (and America) is all about work and working.

On weekends, my parents made up for the day-to-day drudgery of the work week. Saturday was the best, a giant adventure in the Peters household: shopping day. Groceries were a family affair. We'd all hop in the car and head over to IGA or A&P. Dad scoured the papers all week and cut out every coupon he could find. Then we'd go from store to store, buying whatever was on sale at each one.

Next, we'd go to the Dufferin Mall or the Galleria, two west-end, working-class shopping malls, and we'd window-shop for much of the afternoon; my brother and I would head straight to the toy sections of the various department stores. There wasn't the frivolous consumption that we're used to today, but Mom and Dad always made us feel like we had everything. There was never any sense of wanting or doing without. At three in the afternoon, we'd stop at Woolco or at the food court for tea. This was a big deal for Mom and Dad and usually involved a lot of discussion about what they'd have with their tea: Jamaican beef patties, samosas or Maltese pastizzis.

After that, it was time to head home and get ready for Saturday night. There was always something to do or somewhere to go. My parents had a huge circle of extended family and Anglo-Indian friends from back home, so after tea, we'd head home and clean the house if people were coming over or get ready for a night out.

Nothing would make Dad's blood pressure rise more than the task of cleaning. He would kvetch the whole time about this "bloody back-breaking work" with a lot of "damn and blast!", "bloody nuisance," and so on. There was no having to clean up after yourself or vacuum or clean your own bathroom in India. But in Canada, Mom and Dad suddenly found themselves working full time, raising two kids and keeping a house all by themselves. But every Saturday, after the tension-filled cleanathon, everyone would unite when guests started to arrive.

There were friends, and friends of friends; aunts and uncles who were blood-related, and a whole bunch more who weren't but might as well have been. Dad would immediately start to relax as his friends and relatives came over. There were cousins my age, and some older or younger, and we'd tear around the house together while the adults got progressively more drunk. There was always Johnnie Walker Black or Red Label, beer and a ton of food. Sometimes at Uncle Eugene's place, there was a guitar and singing, all of the aunties and uncles belting out the Tom Jones classic "The Green Green Grass of Home" and getting nostalgic for a place they'd never live in again. There was reminiscing about the old days, tinged with the melancholy knowledge that they could never go back, but also a sense of success at having survived and made a new life for themselves here in Canada.

There were jokes, too, usually at somebody's expense, and on the really wild nights, the furniture would be moved out of the way so the dancing could begin. Mom and Dad would break out the vinyl: Frankie Laine, the Platters, Elvis, Engelbert Humperdinck, Tom Jones, Johnny Mathis, Nat King Cole, Cleo Laine, Herb Alpert and the Tijuana Brass, Glenn Miller, Tommy Dorsey, the Mills Brothers, the Ink Spots . . . Dad loved the Ink Spots, especially "To Each His Own," because of how the tenor reached those high notes. He also loved Jim Croce's "Bad, Bad Leroy Brown." But Dad never cared for Sinatra. He felt he was a better actor than a singer, much to the chagrin of Uncle Eardley, Aunty Eileen's husband, who idolized Sinatra.

There was always music playing in our house, and my parents had a real appreciation for the music of their youth. The first record that Dad ever gave Mom was Andy Williams' "Moon River." To this day, my brother has it on his iPod and still gets choked up every time he hears it. The line about two drifters who go off to see the world—that's what really gets him. Of course, my brother gets choked up about anything, whereas I tend to keep things inside more.

I still remember Mom and Dad taking to the living room floor and jiving to Bill Haley and His Comets. They were great dancers together, jiving, waltzing and just having a good time. They took ballroom classes for a while, and even when Dad was in his seventies, he still loved to dance. At weddings and parties, guests would clear the floor to watch Mom and Pop do their thing.

Their favourite song to waltz to was Anne Murray's "Could I Have This Dance." It really was *their* song. When I hosted a fund-raiser for Gilda's Club in 2007, Anne Murray appeared in the show. She started singing "Could I Have This Dance." My brother and I were standing at the side of the stage, and I caught his eye. We were both tearing up. As I read this, I know it sounds pretty gay. But hey, that was Mom and Dad's song, and in that moment, we both knew it. After Dad passed, Mom cut back on going to any functions where there was dancing—it was too much for her to bear without her dance partner.

But back to the parties. This was the time before the extended family drifted apart, as families often do, before uncles and aunties started passing away, and when the novelty of everyone being together here in Canada was still new. One of the topics for the men was politics. The discussions would often get heated: Dad with his leftist, union-oriented, anti-establishment leanings and some of my uncles who were more right wing, pro-American and pro-English. Dad wouldn't hesitate to call them out on their positions and would often suggest that they move to the States if they liked it so much or move back to England if it had been so great. The drinking would continue until it was finally time for the men to eat. Dad wouldn't drink after he ate, so he often had dinner at eleven-thirty or midnight at these functions, his plate piled high with everything being served.

When I think about it, these get-togethers with aunts and uncles, cousins and friends from "back home" was the closest any of them got to going "back home." The men could regain their sense of what it meant to be men—not clerks, salesmen, meat inspectors or assembly-line workers. It was at family functions like these where I first became aware of, well, being aware. I became conscious of

Mikey (left) and me at the cottage.

the idiosyncrasies of my various uncles, their speech patterns, accents—their humour. My cousin Mikey and I would sit around and mimic my dad and my uncles, and laugh hysterically at our imitations. We even started recording them. We would sneak under the dinner table while the men were eating—remember that they'd all been drinking all evening—and tape them while they were talking. Then we'd go off and listen to the tape and perfect our imitations.

If there wasn't a get-together on a Friday or Saturday, Dad would be miserable. He missed the camaraderie of his pals, the interaction and just the opportunity to escape the blood and guts of the slaughterhouse floor.

In the mid-'70s and into the '80s, instead of the Saturday get-togethers, we would often go to a rented cottage on the Trent River with my cousins—Patty (Uncle Arthur's daughter) and her husband, Alex (better know as "Bunty"), and their four boys: Gordon, Bruce, Andrew and Mikey. Mikey was born here, in Toronto, shortly after Patty and Bunty arrived and is the youngest of the four brothers. He's been like a brother to me ever since moving here.

When Patty and Bunty moved to Canada in 1970, we were still living on Indian Road. My dad and brother went to meet the family at the airport, but through some miscommunication they had already left the airport and were waiting for my dad at our house. Gordon, Bruce and Andrew were playing on the street, riding my brother's toy tractor. When one of the neighbours asked where they were from, they said they were Indian. "If you're Indian, who's your chief?" the neighbours asked.

My cousin Mikey and I would sit around and mimic my dad and my uncles, and laugh hysterically at our imitations.

Bunty was crazy strict with the boys as kids and didn't hesitate to pull out his belt and swat them if they got out of line. It seemed over the top to me, even though my own dad was a disciplinarian too. But I guess you need to crack the whip when you've got four boys like that.

Mikey and I would pal around, go out with our dads and Uncle Arthur on one of those aluminum boats, fishing for bass or whatever else we could catch. Most of the time we'd just end up catching sunfish, but we had a great time. Once, Uncle Arthur decided to put one of those aluminum folding lawn chairs with the woven seat and seatback in the boat to sit on. Uncle Arthur, although quite short, was a large man, kind of like my brother, but bald. When I was a kid, I used to think that the Laughing Buddha statue at Patty's house was a statue of Uncle Arthur. Anyway, with the lawn chair in place on the boat, we pulled away from the dock. As soon as Bunty gunned the Johnson outboard, over went the chair, and into the Trent River went Uncle Arthur.

The cottage meant spending time with our dads when they were at their most relaxed, drinking and having a few laughs. Patty was and still is a fantastic cook, and the food was great. Mom didn't care for the cottage life too much. She was a city girl and liked it that way. The sooner we'd get back home, the better for her.

(Back row, from left) Cousin Bruce, my brother, Cousin Andrew, Floyd (*not* a cousin), me (front row, right) and Cousin Mikey.

Mom, Dad and me, relaxing at the cottage.

Much as Dad romanticized his youth hunting and fishing in Burhanpur, I can do the same: from the rented cottage on Trent River to the rented cottage on Blackwater Lake to the cottage that Uncle Arthur bought on Lake Manitouwabing. As kids, we learned how to fish, bait and remove a hook, use a lure and troll. It was all very Canadiana, but with an Indian twist: Patty's fish curry, vindaloos, stir-fries, fish fillets, Uncle Arthur's chapatis that he'd make fresh every morning with fried eggs. All good. We kids would have an entire room to ourselves, with three bunk beds for all of us. We'd stay up late, joking, laughing, farting . . . and making fun of our parents.

CHAPTER 3

SOMEONE WATCHING OVER ME

MY DAD has been—and continues to be—one of the biggest influences on my life. We lost him to cancer on March 15, 2004, a day that is both hard to remember and hard to forget. The only way to really understand me is for you to first get a handle on the force of a man that was my dad.

Eric Peters was fast with his words and quick with his temper. Although he wasn't physically imposing, my father had a strong aura, and he was never one to shy away from an argument. He always felt bad about being such a little guy, but what he lacked in size, he made up for with personality. He was a pint-sized Clint Eastwood—the strong, silent type, always ready to pull the trigger. He wasn't violent, but if he was forced to defend himself, his attacker was in for a surprise. Dad was a fighter by nature and a boxer by training, and if you pushed him hard enough, you'd come to regret it. I have inherited Dad's short fuse—for better and for worse. Dad worked hard to keep his temper in check, and I often find myself having to do the same. Once I lose it, though, I really lose it.

If Dad was pissed off, he wouldn't hesitate to express his displeasure. If he was in the checkout line in a store and things were moving too slowly or someone was trying to butt ahead of him, he'd let fly. When he'd tell us of his altercation, he would describe it this way: "I could see it in the man's face when I asked him what the hell he thought he was doing. I could see he wasn't expecting me to speak English. His mouth fell open—'dah'—you know that blank bloody look these people give you when you challenge them? You see, this is what you have to do. You have to stand up to people like that or they'll walk all over you!"

Dad was always very fussy about his appearance, as am I. He wouldn't step out of the house if his shirt wasn't perfectly pressed. And his hair—or, as we liked to tease him, his *hairs*. He carefully maintained a dozen or so strands in the middle of his scalp. These he grew long, just the way he did when he had a full head of hair back in the '50s and '60s. He'd part the strands dead centre, flip them to each side, and then smooth them back. In his mind, he still had hair like Cary Grant's. In reality, it was closer to Yul Brynner's. I have to admit that I might have inherited a hair obsession from Pop. I've been known to obsess about haircuts and once flew my barber, Frank, from Woodbridge all the way to Vancouver just to give me a haircut before the Juno Awards.

With Dad, it wasn't only the hair. Even in the house, he had to look put together. I can picture him now in his plaid shirt, always over a clean, white undershirt, and his green or white jeans (mind you, he knew to only wear the white ones until Labour Day) with a keychain clipped to one of the belt loops. I would say, "Dad, what are you doing? What's with the keychain?" and he'd answer, "What? It looks good like that." He knew he was taking the piss. He knew he looked a bit silly, but he loved being an original.

He stood straight, chest out, arms back, ready to take on the entire world. And if it was a special night and he and Mom were going out to a dinner or a dance, he'd pull out his best shoes. "Look, I'm wearing my Florsheims!" he'd say, just in case any of us had failed to notice. A quick shine with the horsehair brush, and his burgundy Florsheims were good to go. I can't say I'm different in this respect either. I'm a label whore and I love my shoes. I buy shoes all the time. You'll never catch me wearing sneakers that don't match my jacket, shirt or baseball hat, so don't even try.

Dad was all about tolerance and respect. If somebody was older than you, you had to show them respect. We had this drilled into us from a very young age. If I spoke a certain way to an elder or treated someone older the way I treated others my own age, I could expect to be corrected very quickly, in front of the offended party, or get a quick slap to the head. I was brought

Dad looking good on the dance floor with Mom.

If it was a special night and he and Mom were going out, he'd pull out his best shoes. "Look, I'm wearing my Florsheims!"

up with about a million aunties and uncles whom I wouldn't dare to call by their first names. The protocol when introduced was, "Russell, say hello to Uncle Trevor." "Hi Uncle . . . Yes, Uncle . . . Three bags full, Uncle." For some reason, Canadians were always Mister or Missus, but Anglo-Indians were Auntie and Uncle. If you came to my house as a kid, or even as a young adult, and you called my dad Eric, you'd be corrected immediately: "That's Mr. Peters to you, boy." Call my mom Maureen and she'll ask, "Did we play marbles in the schoolyard together?" Even into my forties, I can't imagine calling some of my friends' parents by their first names, though they ask me to.

My friends thought my dad was hilarious, and they'd rib me all the time about the weird things he'd do, which was easy enough for them since they never had to suffer the consequences. Every day, Mom and Dad would have afternoon tea. This was but one more "Anglo" aspect of their Indian-ness. Usually, they'd have it as soon as they got home from work or, as I mentioned before, as part of their Saturday and Sunday afternoon routine. One day, they were at the mall picking up Jamaican beef patties and sausage rolls to have with their tea and Dad called home to me. "Son," he said, "we're on our way home. Just put the kettle on so when we get home we'll have fresh tea."

I was hanging out with my friends and wanted to do only the bare minimum. I plugged in the kettle, which already had some water in it. Now, it's not like I didn't know better; I knew the importance of four-o'clock tea, but as a kid, I was always looking for the easy way out. My mom and dad came home, made the tea, drank it, and Dad knew right away.

He asked, "Did you *reboil* old water?"

I said, "Yeah."

"You didn't put fresh water?"

"No."

"What the hell's wrong with you?! Are you mildly retarded or something? Too busy acting the fool with your half-wit friends!"

My friends were there, watching all this unfold. They couldn't help but be amused by Dad referring to them as "half-wits" and me as "mildly retarded." They started laughing. I couldn't help it. I started laughing. Then my dad got furious because he thought I was laughing at him, which was disrespectful. "Don't forget yourself, boy!"

Then he started chasing me around the house. I couldn't believe he was so mad about a kettle of water, and I just kept laughing hysterically, and of course that enraged him even more. "Don't you bloody laugh at me, boy!" In the background was my mother yelling at my dad, *"Bus, bus, men!"*—which translates from Hindi as "Enough, enough, men." ("Men" is used by Anglo-Indians, in other phrases too, like "Oof, men!" which is kind of like the Canadian "Oh Christ!" Then there's "Come on, men!" which is like, "Jeez, let's go!")

Once Dad got a good smack in, he was appeased and went back to his tea, grumbling, "These boys forget themselves . . . "—which meant that we'd forgotten our place as children, forgotten to be respectful. Later, we'd have to rehash these sorts of scenes just to make sure I'd understood the lesson. Sometimes I had; sometimes I hadn't. But I always knew that my dad was watching me, making sure I didn't slide into mouthiness.

There was zero room for disrespect. This also applied to disrespecting our mom. If Dad perceived any slight or backtalk at Mom, he'd be all over us. Mom was way more patient, as moms usually are. She'd never rat us out if we'd been rude to her when Dad wasn't around, because she knew there'd be hell to pay. She wanted to avoid having all of Dad's drama in the house. Mom loves dirty jokes, and one of the things we loved about her when we were kids is that she'd actually tell them to us. The funny thing was, Dad's code of respect was so rigid that if Mom "forgot herself" by telling us an off-colour joke, Dad would say, "Maureen!! They're your sons, not your friends. You're their mother, for God's sake!"

One time, when I was about seven, my brother spilled some milk and my dad was spazzing out on him for his "oafishness" and for being a "clumsy fool." For some reason, I wasn't having it; I stepped between them and started yelling and crying, "Don't you hit my brother!" A bit dramatic, I know, but on this particular occasion, I was hell bent on protecting him.

But here's the thing: as much as I joke about getting hit as a child, I can only remember being hit by Dad about three times. I mean, really, if you have to get hit more than three times as a kid and you haven't figured out what you're doing wrong, you're an idiot. I really do believe that kids, especially boys, need a good shot when they get out of line. Those immigrant parents—they've got the right idea.

Of course, Dad did not want to raise idiots, and part of his master plan for us to avoid growing into idiots was teaching us to speak properly. The English language was one of his favourite weapons, and he taught my brother and me how to defend ourselves with it. "Speak clearly!" he'd insist. "Don't mumble, and don't butcher the English language!" God forbid we should stumble over a word or use it incorrectly. Whenever I slipped up or made a mistake with a word, I'd be thinking, "Oh shit . . . Here we go." At the same time, I'd be smiling to myself because I knew what was coming . . . and it was always pretty funny how angry he got. I'd hear, "What the hell's wrong with you? Have you been drinking? Maybe you should stop listening to all that bloody rap music and you'd learn to speak properly!"

I mean really, if you have to get hit more than three times as a kid and you haven't figured out what you're doing wrong, you're an idiot.

I have to hand it to Dad. I first learned to hone a joke and get every word just right because precision with words was drilled into me at an early age. As I get older, I seem to be morphing into my dad. I, too, jump all over people when they misspeak. I can't help it. The funny thing is, I've actually seen my friends shake their heads when I do this and say, "Oh shit . . . Here we go."

My dad was a shameless bargain hunter. I know now that every penny he saved was one he could put towards his family, and this is what motivated him to invent all sorts of crackpot money-saving techniques, including his clever "scratch-and-dent" grocery scheme. He used to take us to this grocery store called Usher's in a seedy neighbourhood in the east end of the city. They had grocery carts full of bashed-up cans and he would always rummage through them. Dented cans or goods with no labels would be marked down with a magic marker. But my dad took these bargains to a whole new level. If he saw something on the shelves that he wanted but that wasn't in the cart, he would happen to drop it—say, for instance, a can of soup—and then bring it to the cashier, saying, "Excuse me, this can is dented. It should be marked down." I don't think we ever had a normal-shaped can in my house, ever. You couldn't stack anything in the cupboards.

My dad's legendary bargain-basement buys extended beyond groceries, once almost costing me my manhood. When I was twenty going on twenty-one, we were living in a bungalow on Epsom Downs Drive in Brampton. (This was my parents' dream home; they always dreamed of living in a bungalow—I don't really know why.) My brother and I had the entire basement to ourselves, with our own bedrooms, a living room, bathroom and side entrance. I was going out with this Indian girl (who shall remain nameless) and it was her first time sleeping over. She was in my bedroom, and I remember I went upstairs to say goodnight to Mom and Dad. Dad pulled me aside and said, "Is she sleeping over?"

"Yes. Is that okay?"

He said, "Yes," and then went to his bedroom.

When I was fifteen he presented me with a book called *What the Swedes Teach About Sex.*

He came back and had something in his palm. Dad shook my hand and he said, "Use this." In my palm he'd placed a red, unlubricated Trojan condom—with 25 cents written on it in magic marker. My dad had bought a *condom* from the scratch-and-dent cart at the Miracle Mart at the Bramalea City Centre. Needless to say, when I tried to get that sucker on that night, I almost took off half my cock. When I couldn't take the pain of it any longer, I had to use the old "I just need to know what you feel like" line.

I don't recall Dad ever having a direct sex talk with me, though when I was fifteen he presented me with a book called *What the Swedes Teach About Sex*. "Here," he said. "Read this." And that was that. There were no pictures, and I never read it. He never followed up ever again, and that book stayed in the drawers of my old bedroom for the longest time—I mean way into my twenties.

*The actual book. I still have it.

Now, I hope you're starting to get a clearer picture of what Eric Peters was like, but to clarify, I'm not saying here that he was weird or cheap. It's more that he was always looking for a good deal and a way to save money. And far from being perfect, my dad was someone who refused to abide by all the conventional rules. He was all about getting ahead, and sometimes that meant breaking the rules for the greater good, so that the underdog had a chance of coming out on top. It might surprise you to know, for instance, that my dad stole—under certain circumstances, he thought this was the right thing to do. He wasn't like a bank robber or anything, but he felt that it was okay to pilfer certain items. He looked at it as though he was sticking it to the man.

So, taking cues from my dad, as I kid I would steal boxing magazines every month from the Hasty Market convenience store—*World Boxing, Ring, KO,* among others. I would even steal comic books and give them to my brother. I was so puny back then that I could stuff them down the front of my shirt. I had a concave stomach, so you couldn't tell they were there.

I remember once when we were at Food City in the Bramalea City Centre—I was probably about eight years old—and my dad pulled a little heist. You might remember that grocers like Food City used to have this system where the clerks would bag your groceries, put the bags in a big plastic basket and run everything outside for you so you could pull up and load everything into your car instead of having to carry it all back to your parking spot. This time, my dad pulled up to grab his groceries and he saw another basket there full of pop, so he grabbed it too and put it in the car. We high-tailed it out of there with a free case of grape pop. Dad always figured that a chain store's margins were big enough to allow for this sort of pilfering. He had a Robin Hood mentality and saw corporate giants as the bad guys who were taking away from the little guy. He'd never hesitate to readjust the scales to balance in the little guy's favour.

Sometimes Dad would send me on shopping errands by myself. I remember he'd tell me to go and buy some pop, but he'd warn me, "Make sure you get the bottle with the most in it!" There I'd be at the store, carefully comparing all the bottles, because in those days they weren't all filled up to the same level. I'd return home and present the bottle of pop to my dad and he would study it.

"Boy, are you blind?" he'd ask. "You've cost us at least an extra glass of pop from this half-filled bottle!" He was prone to exaggeration. The next time we were at Food City, he took me to the pop aisle and showed me the difference between the "half-filled bottle" that I'd brought home and the other "full" bottles. The difference was a matter of centimetres.

"Use your head, not just your eyes," he liked to say.

Dad was a Libra on the cusp of Scorpio. Brother and I are both Libras, too. The symbol for Libra is a scale, like a scale of justice, and for Dad, that was more than a symbol: it was a way of life. From a young age, he instilled in me the notion of justice and the difference between right and wrong. He taught us to question authority. He taught us about South Africa and Nelson Mandela, about India and Gandhi, about Martin Luther King and the civil rights movement. Dad knew what it was like to be the underdog, and he knew firsthand that authority isn't always on the side of good.

He taught me to question authority: "Don't just blindly accept things like a sheep," he'd say. He'd also tell my brother and me never to let the police fingerprint us. He believed the system was weighted against the little guy—whether it was multinational corporations, upper management or the police who wielded the power. "The police are a paramilitary organization that refuse to allow themselves to be questioned by the people they're charged with protecting." He was very skeptical of the police and used to tell us stories about one of his first jobs in Canada, when he worked as a radio dispatcher for the force.

He used to say that if a police officer had accidentally killed somebody innocent, when the body was moved, there'd be half a dozen knives underneath because every cop who'd arrived on the scene would drop a weapon to protect his fellow officer, making the victim look like an aggressor and the police officer look like he'd acted in self-defence. He would hear all the racist chatter over the radio.

There was one time in the '70s when the whole family took a trip to the States, and on the way back, in Princeton, New Jersey, we stopped at a diner. We waited in the lobby for the hostess to seat us, but nobody turned our way. Other people entered after us and they were escorted in immediately. This went on for about forty minutes until it became obvious to Mom and Dad that they weren't being served because of their colour.

My brother wanted to be a radio announcer when he was younger. Dad discouraged him from pursuing this career. He told my brother that, first of all, there wasn't anyone who looked like us in radio and that if my brother did get on the air, he'd have to start out in small towns, and small towns were "no place for us."

When I first told my parents that I wanted to go into comedy, it wasn't a really big deal for them. It's almost like they didn't get it. I might as well have been four years old and saying to my dad that I wanted to be an astronaut. "That's nice, son," he'd say.

Early in my career, my father did try to persuade me away from it. "First of all, son: you're not white, you're not Jewish or even a *nee*-gro." Dad liked to use the word *Negro*, always emphasizing the *ee* sound. He also used to call black people "coloured." He knew these words weren't used anymore, but he loved the wordplay. Using these words was just fun to him.

"Comedy isn't a business for us," he'd say.

I'd counter every reservation Dad had. "That's exactly why I'll make it. There's nobody like me in this business. We're different. *I'm* different."

At that time, Dad was working during the day at a job that he hated, while I was home all day and out all night at gigs and then hanging out with my friends. To this day, the lifestyle of a comic or any other performer is difficult to understand if you've only known a nine-to-five life. To my Dad, doing stand-up didn't sound like work at all. He pictured me hanging out in a nightclub and having a few laughs. He'd see me leaving the house at six or seven at night, heading out for a gig. He'd eye me skeptically. There was always a bit of disappointment as he said goodbye. He worried about me driving at night, and his parting words weren't "Have a good show," but "You be careful on the roads."

Throughout those early years, Dad continued to think my efforts on comedy were wasted. I know that when he died, despite several minor victories in my career along the way, he was still worried about what was to become of me. There was always this sense that he didn't want me to take on something that I might fail at through no fault of

Dad at work in his home office, where he'd often write letters to the editor.

my own. After all, here's a man who had had big dreams too, who had come to Canada thinking he could do better for himself here.

I mentioned earlier that Dad had decided to study journalism shortly after I was born. That's what he ultimately wanted to be: a journalist. He had been writing letters to the editor for a number of years and publishing articles wherever he could, and after finishing his studies in journalism, he put together his portfolio and submitted it to various newspapers in the hope of securing a job. In 1972, he got a call from *The Hamilton Spectator* about an opening for a reporter.

"Mr. Peters, we'd like to see you for an interview," the hiring manager said on the phone. He arrived for his interview and checked in with the receptionist, who asked him to have a seat in the waiting room. The hiring manager appeared and said, "Mr. Peters?" There was no one else in the waiting room. Dad got up and replied, "I'm Mr. Peters." The man looked confused. "I'll be right back," he said, then asked my dad to have a seat and wait another minute. The man returned a few moments later and said to Dad, "The position's been filled." As far as my dad was concerned, it was a lie. He knew that his colour was the real reason he was being denied an interview. He never rebounded from this humiliation.

Remember that at this time, when you turned on the TV, all you saw was a sea of white faces. It was a different world from the one we now live in, where we see news reporters of every shade and colour—brown faces, black faces and Asian faces. Of course, there are still some weird exceptions in the media, even today. Just look at how long it took for *ER* to cast an Indian doctor. And *Grey's Anatomy* still doesn't have one. When was the last time you went into a hospital and *didn't* see an Indian doctor?

In my dad's mind, the message he got from the media was "We don't see you" and "You don't belong here." There was no one out there I could point to and say, "Look, Dad. That guy looks just like us, and look what he did!" The closest comparisons we had were black entertainers like Redd Foxx, Sidney Poitier, Bill Cosby, Flip Wilson and Ben Vereen.

Because of Dad's disappointment at not being able to achieve his dream of becoming a journalist and at having to do blue-collar work with a white-collar mindset, he never wanted my brother or me to feel that disappointment. He found strength in the union that he worked for. "Son, you should get a union job. There's the Chrysler plant, there's Dominion Glass, there are the airlines, Canada Customs. These companies pay very well and the union will protect you." These were the same kinds of jobs that Anglo-Indians had enjoyed back in India, and Dad saw them as the best options for his sons. There was always the sense that Dad wanted to keep the bar low for my brother and me, to protect us from unfairness.

After seeing one of my early TV specials, I remember asking Dad, "So, did you like it?" He was quiet for a bit and then said, "You seem to only do jokes about a few things."

"I only do jokes about what I know, Dad."

Then he said, "You should expand your repertoire like the other comics, do the same topics they do." So I responded by saying that I didn't want to do what everyone else was doing.

"Well," he said, "maybe you should start reading *Reader's Digest*. They have good jokes in there, things you can talk about."

Dad died exactly one month and one day after my infamous *Comedy Now!* special on TV. I remember my parents watching it for the first time in the family room. Mom was laughing her head off, and Dad was watching her with this funny look on his face. Then he said, "You're really a fan of this guy. You really find him funny, don't you?" Mom said, "Of course I do. He's my son." And even though Dad was being a bit of a smart-ass, I could see then that his mindset about my work was starting to change. In his own way, he was proud of me.

Immediately after Dad had passed, my world began to change radically and my career really took off. I don't want to get all weird and superstitious, but I honestly felt that my dad had a hand in those changes. I believe that my father—his spirit—is a guardian angel that helped me make it to where I am today. I believe my dad has been beside me in spirit during all of the pivotal moments in the last five years of my life.

I'll let you in on a secret: I have a little ritual I perform every night before I go onstage. I talk to my dad. Backstage, when others think I'm blabbing to myself or reviewing the set, what I'm actually doing is talking to him. When I get goose bumps, that's Dad responding—that's when I know he's there with me. And if I don't get goose bumps, I start to panic. Sometimes, I'll start talking to him and at first I'll feel

I believe my father—his spirit—is a guardian angel that helped me make it to where I am today.

nothing, and then I'll think, *Where are you?* I start to wonder if he's abandoned me and I'm out there all alone. It's not a good feeling to have just before you're about to perform in front of a sold-out house of cheering fans. I always get the goose bumps back, though, and then I can relax. Every time, I think to myself, *Thank God he's back.* And knowing he's there with me, knowing I'll be okay out in front of the crowd, that means I'm ready to take the stage.

I'm not religious at all. Technically, I'm Catholic, but the older I get, the less I see the point of organized religions. I see myself as more of a spiritual guy, and I really feel that people know what's right and what's wrong in this world—they should know what to do and what not to do to people. I'm not saying that I always do what's right or that I've always been good to people. I haven't. And believe me: if there's anything Catholic about me, it would be the guilt that I feel for the things that I have done wrong in my life. For me, Dad's my guardian angel, and I feel like all my successes are his responsibility. He's caused all of these good things from the other side. I can almost hear him negotiating with St. Peter up in heaven: "Here, St. Peter . . . Let's just make sure that the Air Canada Centre shows are bloody well sold out. Make sure you look after my son!"

After Dad died, for a while I stepped back from using a lot of the stories about him. They were hitting a little too close to home for me, but I'm finding that as time passes, I can bring him back into my act as a celebration of who he was and what he meant to me—what he still means to me. In the fall of 2005, during my first solo national tour of Canada, we did a show at the North York Centre for the Performing Arts on October 23, my dad's birthday. This was the first time I was headlining my own tour and it was a big deal for me. The show was great and I was relieved that it had gone well in front of the hometown crowd. I ended the show with my "Somebody Gonna Get a-Hurt Real Bad" routine and the audience was on its feet. I looked skyward and then said into the mike, "Happy Birthday, Dad!" I knew he was right there with me that night.

I still have communion with my dad, even when I'm not going onstage. When I'm driving, sometimes I'll play the Platters or the Ink Spots and have a talk with Dad. A couple of Christmases before Dad died, my brother gave him a CD of Paul Robeson, the baritone concert singer and union movement activist. Dad was a big fan of his, not only because of his voice but because he was such a strong civil rights activist and had spoken up against racial segregation and fascism all through his life. Dad put on the CD, and soon after, he excused himself from Christmas-morning breakfast and retreated upstairs. We soon realized it was because he was crying. When he came back down, my brother said, "Dad, I got you the CD because I thought you'd like it." Dad was really quiet, and Brother asked him, "What's wrong, Dad?"

"It just reminds me of my father . . . " he said quietly. Thirty-five years since his own father had passed, and he still missed him to the point of tears.

Sometimes I think about the things Dad used to tell me, and they mean more to me now than they ever did when he was alive. My father had one big regret when he was dying. "I have nothing to leave you guys and I'm sorry," he'd say. And I'd try to tell him that he had never let us down, never. I used to say, "You got hustled, Dad. It's not like you gambled with your money. It's not like you weren't trying to save up for us. You did your best."

Around the late '80s and early '90s, Dad was duped in a real estate scheme along with a whole bunch of other family members, including my cousins, my aunts and friends. They'd invested in a strip plaza near Ottawa and were making collective payments toward the mortgage. They had signed personal guarantees for this "great real estate investment." Everything seemed to be fine, until the bank contacted the investors and advised them that they were in default on the mortgage payments. Dad later learned that what were supposed to be mortgage payments had actually been used to pay management fees. The group had been swindled and Dad ended up losing $250,000, his entire life's savings. We even had to sell our house on Epsom Downs Drive to pay for his portion of the debt.

My dad wept as he locked the door of that house for the last time. I can see him now with our cat, Billy, in his arms. He looked doddering and confused. He said he was an utter failure to the family, and there was nothing we could do or say to convince him otherwise. We became renters again for the first time in two decades, moving from owners of a house in the E-section of Bramalea down to renters in the N-section of town. (Bramalea neighbourhoods are grouped alphabetically. The streets in each neighbourhood start with the same letter. In the E-section, we lived on Epsom Downs; in the N-section, we lived on Newbridge.) Twenty years of my parents' hard work had evaporated right before their eyes. What hurt my dad the most was that he'd been scammed, not by an anonymous huckster or an institution, but by a friend—the best man at his wedding and my very own godfather.

At the age of sixty-six, after spending only one year in retirement, my dad had to go back to work. It was a really bad time for the whole family, and it broke my heart to see Dad waking up early in the morning and going to his shitty job as a federal meat inspector in a stinking processing plant. My father was proud and practical, and he never backed away from doing whatever work he had to in order to keep a roof over our heads. Within two years, he'd saved enough to buy another house.

When Dad was sick, there came a point when we knew it was coming to the end of the road. We spent all of our time trying to keep everything around him peaceful, to make sure there was no drama—which wasn't always easy. He could be pretty cranky some days after going through the indignity of full-body radiation. We did whatever we could to make him comfortable—good booze, good dinners at home, good restaurants—and that's why I have no regrets. Some people who've been through this might wish their loved one had lived longer or would wish their dad could be seeing what they're seeing, experiencing what they're experiencing. But I feel lucky for what I got, for having my father as long as I did and for feeling such a strong connection with him even after he's gone.

I also feel like I had the best closure with him out of everyone in my family. The weekend he died, I was doing a gig at Yuk Yuk's in Ottawa. My mom and my brother had spent most of Friday and Saturday with Dad at the hospital. Family and friends had dropped by to see him as well. He had even asked Mom to make him some mince curry, daal and rice, which he ate. My mom and brother spent all of Sunday afternoon and evening with Dad. He was tired but seemed stable when they left to go for dinner at Red Lobster on Queen Street in Brampton. Brother got back to our place in Woodbridge at around ten-thirty that night. An hour later, Mom called him and said that she got a call from the hospital telling her to come back. They were all back to the hospital by eleven-thirty. Dad's condition had completely changed. He now wore an oxygen mask and was unintelligible.

I was already on my way back home from Ottawa after the show, at around two-thirty in the morning, when my brother called on my cell. His voice was quiet and calm.

"Brother," he said, "instead of heading home, just drive straight to the hospital, okay?" My stomach dropped. I knew what that meant.

"Okay," I said.

"And Brother?" he added. "Don't speed."

Of course, my brother had waited until after my show to call. He knew that the show would have ended at around eleven, and by the time I'd left the club, it would be midnight. He'd then calculated exactly when to reach me so that I wouldn't start speeding the second I got on the highway. At this point, I was on Highway 401 near Port Hope, Ontario. My girlfriend, Shivani, was with me. I hung up the phone and didn't say a word. All I could think of was that I needed to get to the hospital right away. I had my suspicions, but in my head, my dad was indestructible. I told myself that he might have taken a turn for the worse, but it wasn't really going to be the end.

Brampton was about two hours away, but I made it to the hospital in fifty minutes. I was doing about 180 kilometres per hour the whole way. These days, they would take my car away and throw me in jail for that. But at the time, I didn't care. I needed to see my dad.

When I arrived at the hospital, Mom and Brother were there. They told me Dad had been in and out of consciousness. Mom said that in between my father's drifting, he would open his eyes, look up at her and say, "Where's Russell?"

"He's on his way," she told him.

He pulled his mask away and managed to say, "Tell Russell not to speed. Tell him not to drive fast." He just kept saying that to her as I was on my way there, as if he knew exactly what I was doing, as if he'd already been travelling in and out of body.

I went into Dad's room, and the moment I saw him there, lying still on the bed, I started bawling. He looked terrible. He was wheezing and could hardly breathe. Every now and then he'd sit up and try to take his oxygen mask off. I'd never seen him like that before. I knew this was it. For a while, he kept saying, "Arthur, Arthur, no. No, Arthur." He was talking to his older brother who had passed away years earlier.

After some time passed, Dad's condition started to improve slightly and he looked a little better. At around six in the morning, because Dad was doing okay, we told my brother to go home and get some rest. And so, we sent him on his way, thinking there was still time. My mom and Shivani were hungry, so they went to McDonald's to get some breakfast.

It was very close to dawn, and I sat alone with my dad. Now, bear in mind that he hadn't said a word to me at all. He was barely aware that anybody was even there with him. He was out cold. I sat down beside him and grabbed his hand in the quiet, and as soon as everybody was gone, out of nowhere, his voice came out clear, confident, strong.

"How were your shows?" he asked.

I was shocked, but I answered, "They were good, Dad. The audience asked about you."

"How's the weather out there today?" he went on, as though it were just an ordinary morning between the two of us.

"It's shitty outside, Dad. You're better off in here."

And then we fell asleep together like that, still holding hands. My mom came in later and we both woke up. I told her that I had talked to him, that we'd had a perfectly lucid and crystal-clear conversation.

At 7 A.M., the nurses changed shifts and one of them gave my dad a pill or something, and I remember he couldn't even chew. The staff said they were going to transfer him from Brampton to Hamilton for his scheduled radiation. I was like, "What the fuck?"

The family all got out of the way, and we stood outside the door. I just stood there, watching from the doorway, as the nurse tried to move my dad. I went in to help, and he was standing now and he wet himself; he couldn't help it. He looked right at me then, with a look that said, "I'm not living like this." All of a sudden, I saw his eyes change colour; they were turning yellow. Something was wrong. Then, just before he closed his eyes, there was a very clear moment when he said goodbye. It was all there in his eyes: "I love you, bye." And then one of the nurses started yelling, "Code blue! Code blue!" Everybody ran in and it was complete chaos. More nurses, more staff were pushing past, furious and frantic. But that was the end. He died right then and there.

My mom had been just outside the door, just a few feet away. She could have had that last moment with him, but it happened with me, kind of a last hurrah that he saved for his baby. It was a horrible day, and it's still hard to relive the memory. It's not like I play this over in my head a lot, but sometimes when I watch a movie or something and there's a father-and-son scene, I get really emotional—even by the weirdest, most ridiculous thing, like the movie *Click* with Adam Sandler. It's about this guy who has a remote control for his life so he can fast-forward and rewind to all of the good parts. Sandler fast-forwards so far that he misses his father's death. Suddenly he realizes this and asks himself, "When was the last time I saw my dad?" Christopher Walken's character, who's kind of his guide with this remote control, rewinds Sandler back to the last time he was with his dad. In the scene, Sandler just brushes his dad off . . . and then never sees him again. I started bawling in the theatre at that scene.

As I'm writing this, I'm finding it hard to talk about Dad in the past tense, because my feelings for him are as alive as they've always been, and even though he's gone, there's a part of him that's always with me. I really love my dad.

After Dad's passing, I used to dream about him—a lot, almost every night. I would be standing outside an old hospital, the kind with frosted-glass windows through which you could see shapes and figures moving. Then I'd be inside, standing at the door of a room in the hospital, and I would hear my mom crying. I'd walk in, and my dad would be lying there, and the minute I arrived he would sit up and he'd say, "It's okay. I'm fine." When I woke up from these dreams, I'd be freaking out, and of course I'd miss him even more.

Then, about four or five months later, I had a different dream about him. My dad really liked the restaurant Tucker's Marketplace because it was a buffet and you could eat everything there—roast beef, piles of shrimp and seafood, a hundred different desserts. In my dream, my dad is at Tucker's, and he says to me, "Look at where I am! I'm in the best place I've ever been. I have the best food . . . Look, all my friends are here." I see his pal Uncle Edgy, who passed suddenly a few years earlier. "We're all having a great time," Dad says. "I'm in paradise." He kept repeating that in the dream: "I'm in paradise." *Great,* I'm thinking to myself in the dream, *Dad's died . . . and become a Muslim.* "Don't worry about me anymore, son," Dad says. "I'm the happiest I've ever been." And then I wake up.

"I'm in paradise." He kept repeating that in the dream: "I'm in paradise." *Great,* I'm thinking to myself in the dream, *Dad's died . . . and become a Muslim.*

Since that time, I have never dreamt about my father again. Never. It was as if, after five months of mourning, he was putting me out of my own torment. He was saying, "Look, I'm okay. I'm still there for you. I know what you're doing." It kind of pissed me off, because I wanted to dream about him again. I don't see him anymore in dreams, and it really bothers me that I don't. It's been years, and I would really like to have just one dream about him so he could let me know he's still there.

I talked to a family friend, Bob Houston, about these dreams. Bob was a very good friend of Dad's and also happens to be a dream analyst. He's someone Dad always really looked up to. They'd go drinking together on occasion and Bob, a great sports and boxing fan, used to love watching fights with Dad. He was gutted when Dad died.

So I asked Bob about the Tucker's dream, and right away, he asked me, "What was your dad wearing in the dream?" I said he was wearing light-coloured clothing, very light-coloured clothing. "Good," Bob said. "That's very good." Apparently, the darker the clothing, the more the spirit is in limbo, whereas light clothing suggests the soul has arrived. This sounds pretty trippy, I know, but I can't tell you how good it was to hear this. My dad's not a lost soul. He's out there in Tucker's Marketplace paradise, and he's doing just fine.

CHAPTER 4

THE BROTHERS PETERS

I'VE GOT ONE BROTHER, just one: Clayton. It feels really strange to even refer to him as Clayton because I never, ever call him by his name and he never calls me by mine. There's something about using our actual names that sounds disrespectful. Dad's nickname for me was Cunchi-pops. It's a made-up name, and I don't even know where it came from. It was originally Mom's nickname for Dad. Mom ended up using Cunchi-pops to refer to both Dad and myself. Dad also called me Susu Pot, which basically means pisspot. I just called Dad "Dad" or Pops—or, if I was feeling dangerous, Eric. But whenever I called him by his actual name, he'd just growl back at me, "Hmmm . . ." Dad just called Mom "Mom" and by her name, Maureen, but he seemed to place the emphasis on the "Mo" part. It sounded more like "*Mo*-reen."

My dad's nickname for my brother was Walker. Dad originally wanted to call my brother Clint, after the '60s cowboy actor Clint Walker. Clint Walker was apparently over six feet tall, and Dad thought my brother was never going to be that tall, so he decided to go with Clayton instead. This name change didn't stop him from referring to my brother as Walker for the rest of his life. He also called him Wapiti, after the elk—I think he just liked the sound of the word *Wapiti* and the alliteration with Walker.

These days, I call my brother Brother or Toots or Teets—and he calls me the same things. Toots and Teets come from the George Carlin bit "Seven Words You Can Never Say on Television" from his *Class Clown* album. The other part of this bit that we appropriated is Tater Tits, or just plain Tits. That's right, sometimes I call my brother Tits. Occasionally, I even call him Tits McGee, from *Anchorman: The Legend of Ron Burgundy*.

Before all of the "Teeting," we called each other Gay, as in "Hey Gay, what are you doing?" Now, using *gay* like this doesn't mean we're homosexuals or even homophobic—nothing could be further from the truth. It's just one of those dumb things that you start out saying and it sticks. Sometimes, even now, we'll be in a store or something, and my brother will be trying to get my attention, and he'll yell out, "Hey Gay! Look at this!" Obviously, we feel like idiots when we suddenly realize there are other people around. But somehow, you can't stop a nickname once it starts.

My earliest memories of my brother are of him giving me baths when I was three or four years old—how's that for "gay"? Because he was six years older than me, and both of us were latchkey kids, Brother was responsible for making sure that I was okay from the time he was about ten years old. I remember that, even back then, he was always doing things to make me laugh. In the bathtub, he would cover my head and face with bubbles and make me look like a dog with foamy ears; I would laugh hysterically at just about everything he did.

When I was in senior kindergarten, my brother would take me to and from school every day. We used to cross the "creek" behind the greenbelt and townhouses where we lived—it was actually a storm drain overflow—and the trick was to run down the banks of the creek (it wasn't very wide) and leap across to the other side. Some days it would rain and the creek would become impassable, but at this time, it wasn't a heavy flow. My brother made me go first, and I made it to the other side. Then I was waiting for my brother to cross, and I don't know what happened next, but suddenly he slipped and ended up on his ass, backwards in the creek, completely sprawled out—spread-eagled and everything. I was killing myself laughing. It was like Lee Majors in *The Fall Guy*. This is my first recollection of me laughing my ass off. To this day, the memory still makes me laugh. My brother wasn't hurt, but I was sure he was going to get mad at me for laughing. He didn't, though. He was cool about it.

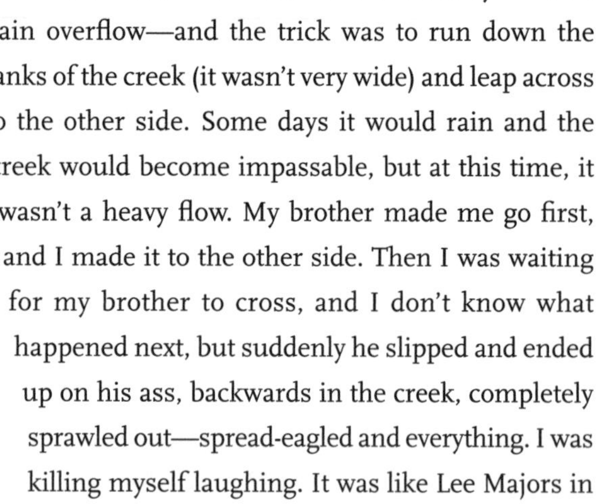

When I was young, I idolized Brother. He seemed to have it all under control. He was always reading and would sometimes sit at the table and draw. I was blown away by what he put on the page. I always thought to myself, *Wow, I can't draw at all, and here's my brother, with all this talent.* When he was fourteen and fifteen, he knew cool, older black guys with these huge Afros, guys who introduced him to funk—stuff like "One Nation Under a Groove" by Funkadelic and "Ready or Not" by Herbie Hancock. At the time, these songs were meaningless to me, but years later I would realize what important classics they were. Music really seemed to be the thing that connected Brother to people he knew—which I guess is true for a lot of kids in their teens.

In his later teens, my brother suddenly became Joe Popular. As a kid, I was blown away by all the friends he had, from all backgrounds. At one point, he was hanging out with this guy Marco, who had this huge '74 Monte Carlo. He'd pull up at the house to pick up my brother and there'd be like two or three girls in the back of the car. It looked awesome to me! Remember that I was this super-skinny, small kid who was only eleven or twelve at this time. Brother was eighteen and had been lifting weights for a while, and in keeping with the fashion of the time, when *Flashdance* was big, he'd cut off the sleeves and collars of his sweatshirts, showing off what seemed to me, a gangly twelve-year-old, like enormously huge arms.

A six-year age difference in your teens seems like a lifetime. We didn't hang out together or share friends—all he was interested in was hanging out with his friends and, of course, chasing chicks, and I was just some little kid. He really didn't want me underfoot, and I was an annoying pain in the ass. However, he was the quintessential big brother, leading the way and looking out for little Russell who was growing up behind him.

Unlike other sibling relationships I've seen, ours was pretty steady, perhaps because of the age difference between us. When I was in grade school, Brother always had my back, and that remains true to this day. During the years when I would get beat up all the time, I would sometimes run home right before a bully got to me. Before

"If you don't leave me alone, I'm going to tell my brother!"

leaving, I'd issue my big threat: "If you don't leave me alone, I'm going to tell my brother!" My brother was bigger than anyone at school, so this usually worked quite well. And apart from being a big kid physically, Brother had this way of walking that deterred anyone from taking him on—much like my dad. If somebody so much as tried, all he'd have to do was grab the little punk by the shirt collar and give him a warning, and the trouble would be over. I saw him rise to my defence on more than one occasion, and it did wonders in making me feel better and safer.

When I was going to Chinguacousy Secondary School in Brampton, there were these two Italian guys who were giving me a hard time, so I told my brother about them. The next day, he showed up at the school and stood outside the guys' classroom, waiting for them to leave. They recognized my brother because he was friends with their brothers back in the day. He told them I was his little brother and that nobody should be bothering me, especially not them. They were always very respectful after that.

Me, and my brother looking like a retarded Lou Ferrigno.

Brother is an intelligent guy, always has been, and because of that, he's hardly ever been in a physical altercation in his life. Like my dad, he's got an incredible power with words, and most of the time, that's all you need. Admittedly, Brother and I argued on a few occasions. But there's one argument that grew into a full-blown fight. I was fifteen at the time, and Brother did something that made me furious. Interestingly, I now have no recollection about what it is that he did. Anyhow, typical of me at the time, I lost it. I ended up yelling and grabbing a hammer, which I flung at him. Fortunately, he's pretty good on his feet, and he ducked fast, resulting in the hammer striking the wall and leaving a rather noticeable hole. As soon as I did it, I thought to myself, *Aw, what the hell did I do that for?* But it was too late. I'd done it. Our argument was pretty much over at that point, because I had to high-tail it out of the house before my dad saw the gaping hole. To this day, I still don't even know what made me so angry that I reacted like that. I still feel a little remorse, but as it turns out, my brother doesn't even remember this incident. Anyhow, you can't let that kind of thing fester when you've only got one brother in the whole world. My dad used to tell us, "After our balls close, it's just going to be the two of you. You have to look after each other." He was talking about *eye*balls, by the way . . .

I lost it. I ended up yelling and grabbing a hammer, which I flung at him.

During my teen years, there were some ups and downs, the usual big-brother-to-little-brother stuff—"Turn that music down!" "Tell your friends not to park in the driveway!"—but things changed in the summer of 1989. Our whole family had gone to England for an Anglo-Indian reunion, a get-together of AI's from all over the world. This was the first one ever held. My whole family was staying at Uncle Ron and Aunty Val's house in South Harrow. There were so many of us that my mom and dad were staying in my cousins Darren and Charlene's room, while they in turn were sleeping on the floor of their parents' room. My brother and I slept on the foldout couch in the family room.

Late one night, my brother and I were listening to this London radio station. They were playing some really wicked music—a lot of it house music, which I was just starting to get into (since my brother was always playing it at home). We were lying there listening, and suddenly this song came on that didn't sound like anything we'd heard before—ambient, mellow, smooth, with a synthesized sax sound and great highs and percussion. It was "Pacific State" by 808

State. This was the first song that we really bonded to. We both loved it, and it was kind of like I was leaving behind a certain amount of rebelliousness against my brother and our worlds were starting to come together again.

Music is really important to me, just as it was to my parents. In the late '70s, my brother used to babysit me on Saturday nights if our parents went out. He'd listen to disco and funk on WBLK out of Buffalo. I pretended wasn't really into all that—"More Bounce to the Ounce" by Zapp, "Bounce, Rock, Skate, Roll" by Vaughan Mason & Crew, "Christmas Rappin'" by Curtis Blow. Around that time and into the early '80s, I started getting into Iron Maiden, Led Zeppelin and AC/DC. I was already into KISS, since '77. In 1979, when Mom and I returned from a trip to India, my dad and brother met us at the airport. Brother was all excited because he had bought the twelve-inch single of "I Was Made for Loving You" by KISS (their "disco" song), and he knew how much I loved them. He was now part of a DJ crew called Musique. He started playing mixed tapes at around this time, and I'd yell out to him, "Turn that disco shit off!" Truth be told, I actually liked funk and disco, but didn't want him to know. In 1981, my brother started getting into New Wave—bands like Duran Duran, Spandau Ballet and Haircut 100. They all sounded a bit disco-y, but they were all made up of white guys from England. I dug in my heels. I remember asking him, "What? Now you're turning into a white boy?" I was a total hypocrite: I was listening to KISS and other all-white rock bands—not exactly world music.

Yes, this is me.

Anyhow, on that summer night in London, ten years after he played the KISS twelve-inch for me, something clicked between us. For the rest of the trip, we searched for an 808 State album and kept an eye out for the video for "Pacific State." It was an important milestone for both of us.

Around 2000, my brother and I decided—at the tender ages of thirty and thirty-six—to move out. We bought a townhouse together on Piazza Crescent in Woodbridge. My brother found the place while I was away at the Edinburgh Festival in Scotland. Initially we were going to buy it through a rent-to-own program, but Dad didn't feel comfortable with that. He thought that paying more than $200,000 for a townhouse was crazy. "There are much cheaper ones here in Brampton!" Even so, he helped us out with the down payment. My brother put down the bulk of it and I was mostly responsible for making sure that I put enough into the "house account" we set up to cover the monthly mortgage and utility payments. It was a dope little townhouse—still is. We moved in in January 2001, and then my brother took off on me seven years later 'cause he fell in loooooove with my awesome now-sister-in-law, Emma (or Ellie May or "Sisters," as I call her).

Brother changed jobs that year to what he thought would be one with better long-term opportunities, as an international contracts manager for an oil and gas pipeline company in Rexdale. There was only one problem: He hated it. He realized it wasn't for him when, at the company sales and marketing meeting, held about four weeks after he started, the guys he worked with told him about their initiation program. He was supposed to wear a beanie with a propeller on it for the entire week of the sales meeting. This might be okay for a bunch of engineering-school frat boys, but that's not my brother. Like my dad, he believes in dignity and self-respect. When he told them he wouldn't do it, he effectively became an outcast. He hated every minute of the four years he spent working there.

Me holding my umbrella and trying to keep my pants up (what did you *think* I was doing??), my sister-in-law, Emma, and my brother on their wedding day.

I was flat broke and barely making house payments, my brother was working a job he hated, and then my father was diagnosed with a form of skin cancer.

It was 2002 at this point, I was flat broke and barely making house payments, my brother was working a job he hated, and then my father was diagnosed with a form of skin cancer, mycosis fungoides. Dad was pissed. "All this time and this is what gets me?!" He was determined to fight, and we came together as a family to help him do that.

It was an awful time. Dad was such a proud man, and the diagnosis hit him hard for lots of reasons. Even before he was diagnosed, he knew something was wrong. He would describe this itch just below his skin, an itch he'd never be quite able to scratch. He'd rub lotion on his arms to help soothe the sensation, but the itching never went away. Later, when the disease progressed, he became obsessed with his skin and how it would flake off. I think he felt like he was losing pieces of himself, and for a man like my father, someone who had an extra awareness of his skin and its colour, this disease offered another layer of cruelty.

Going into 2003, doctors advised Dad to get a special type of blood treatment that was being done in Philadelphia. The treatment was being paid for by OHIP (the Ontario Health Insurance Plan), but the travel and hotel weren't. For a while, Brother and I were financing Mom and Dad's six-hundred-dollar flights to the hospital in the States, which was a huge amount for both of us, as it is for most people. At the same time that this was happening, I was going to shoot an independent film in the States. We would start in January, and the shoot would last three months. I cleared out my schedule of live shows, cancelled any gigs and didn't book any new ones until the movie was supposed to be completed. I was going to get paid what was good money at the time—fifteen grand. I'd even turned down hosting *The Toronto Show*, a talk-variety TV program on the fledgling Toronto 1 channel, to do the movie. Suddenly, just before we were supposed to start shooting in New Jersey, there was a problem with the film's financing and it was going to be delayed for three months. I scrambled to take on any gigs that I could, just so I could pay for my car, my share of the mortgage and, if possible, help Mom and Dad with their travel. Three months came and went, and the shoot was again delayed three months. Again, a mad scramble to pick up any gigs that I could. I was taking it in the hoop financially and was making very little money.

Ultimately, the movie never happened. It took me nine months to figure that out. It couldn't have happened at a worse time. I had just enough to make car payments, and barely enough for my share of the mortgage. We got behind on our property taxes and even had our gas turned off once. My brother was doing the best he could, but it took a lot to cover one household, let alone help out Mom and Dad at the same time. When we could no longer afford to fly my parents to Philadelphia, we resorted to driving them back and forth—desperate road trips with the singular goal of continuing Dad's treatment. The trip was nine or ten hours each way, and nobody in that car complained.

Well, that's not actually true. After eight or nine hours of driving, Dad would start to get very antsy. This was spring, and the clocks hadn't sprung ahead yet, so it was still dark early in the evening, and as the sun set and the darkness came down, Dad's mood would shift. We'd be somewhere on the interstate in Pennsylvania, still a ways from Philly, and Dad would become increasingly frustrated that we all had to go through this.

When Dad was upset, the whole car would go quiet. We'd try to take his mind off things by playing music he liked—music we all liked, actually. We'd play anything from '60s lounge music—Andy Williams, Burt Bacharach, Glen Campbell, Tom Jones—to Dad's perennial favourites, the Platters and the Ink Spots. Mom would be there, too, trying to keep things lighthearted and jolly, as is her way. She actually enjoyed the road trips. They reminded her of our family trips in the '70s to Myrtle Beach, New York, Washington and Pennsylvania. We were all doing our best.

When we'd finally see the sign for Philadelphia, everyone would finally relax. We would arrive at the Holiday Inn Express on Walnut Street and go to this little corner store to pick up a six-pack of beer for dad. Dad would unwind with a beer in the hotel room, then we'd go out as a family for some Indian food at a buffet across the street. Dad would have another drink there, and slowly, he'd start to settle in.

The next morning, bright and early, he would start his treatment in the University of Pennsylvania Hospital. This was a beautiful hospital—it even had a valet—but Dad hated being there. We'd sign Dad out in the evenings, go out for drinks and then have a nice meal. It was a good way to keep everyone's spirits up as best we could. One of the things that really bothered him was that the chemo and all the other treatments made him lose his sense of taste. He was a man who loved food—it was one of his great passions—but the more treatment he received, the less he could enjoy it.

On the drive back home to Toronto after Dad's treatment, he'd have to wear large, black sunglasses and we'd have to put towels over the windows of the car to protect him from the sun. Post-treatment, his skin became more sensitive to light. In the darkened car, we'd make our way home quietly, but as we crossed upstate New York, Dad's frustration would rise again. We'd say, "Pop, don't worry. There's nothing you can do. It's not like you asked for this to happen." On one of the trips, we stopped at a Starbucks for coffee. My brother had ordered a Frappuccino and Dad asked for a sip.

All in all, those drives weren't that terrible. Brother was taking Mondays and Fridays off from work to do the trips, and I wasn't taking weekend gigs. We bonded as a family and had a lot of time to say everything we needed to say to each other—and for that, I'm grateful.

That's really the only upside to our father's death and how he died: we had two full years to say all the things we wanted to say to him and do all the things we wanted to do with him. We got to tell Dad that we loved him. We got to tell him that he had done all the right things for us and that he should have no regrets. There were quiet times when it would be only the two of us. We'd watch boxing together on TV, and just sit there holding hands. Dad got to see us as grown men, as men who had learned respect, had never broken the law or gone to jail and who held family as sacred. "You've got to look out for each other, no matter what," he told Brother and me. He also told us how proud he was of us. That's something you can never forget.

He also told us how proud he was of us. That's something you can never forget.

My brother and I have often noted that my dad was tough to like as a younger man, but easy to love as an old man. In pictures when he was young, Dad looked like a bit of a dick. If we'd known him then, I don't think we would have liked him. And of course, he was tough on us growing up; he was a disciplinarian and he kept us in line. But as an old man, he was fantastic. He fell into that role wonderfully.

We've had a couple of other family members pass away suddenly, including my cousin Andrew, who was murdered in the Dominican Republic in 1995, as well as several aunts and uncles, and what you immediately realize once you hear the news is that you'll never have a chance to say goodbye. It wasn't like that with Dad.

My dad was always a scotch drinker, and he loved Johnnie Walker Red, so when Dad was sick, Brother and I decided we'd treat him to the best (and most expensive) scotch whisky we could: Johnnie Walker Blue Label. Dad loved it. When we presented the bottle to him, his eyes lit up. He gave us a look as if to say "You shouldn't have," but you could tell he was completely ecstatic about having that bottle in his hands. As a man who had always put his family first, it was unimaginable that he would have shelled out over two hundred dollars for a bottle of booze. He set out to drink it right away. He made his first toast "To my sons," raising a glass to us. Then he said, "No one but me is going to touch this bottle, and I'm only going to drink it on special occasions." And so, over the span of about a year, Dad would pour himself a glass of Blue Label at Christmas, Easter or on one of our birthdays.

My dad died on March 15, 2004, after one hell of a fight.

He made it quite ceremonial, and he'd always toast to our health. Looking back, I'm not sure who enjoyed that bottle more—Dad, who loved the scotch, or the rest of us, who loved to watch him drink it. When he got sicker, Dad decided, "I'm not leaving this bottle for anybody else. I'm finishing it off before I go." And he did.

My dad died on March 15, 2004, after one hell of a fight. About a year after Dad's passing, everything changed for my brother and me. Brother's workplace had become even more toxic. It got to the point where a few of his not-so-pleasant colleagues even accused him of taking kickbacks. If you knew my brother personally, you'd realize just how ridiculous the accusation was.

He'd come home and tell me about these things, and I'd be pissed. Things had changed radically for me; not only was I beginning to taste success, I was making my first excursions into the States. My brother and I had a habit of talking to each other at least once a day by phone. Our household schedule was completely reversed; he'd leave in the morning and then come home in evening at around seven or eight, by which time I'd already be out for a gig or to hang out with my friends. However, at the same time as the changes taking place in my career, he was also becoming more of a confidant I'd seek out to discuss everything that was happening. He was tracking the new trajectory of where things were going for me, sometimes staying at work until 9 P.M. to work on my calendar and review all my travel arrangements. This was all new to both of us, but there he was, not only excited about the new opportunities but concerned about my safety and security on these new U.S. shows with unknown promoters.

We were still grieving the loss of our father and were coming out of hard financial times. We drew on each other for support. The few times we couldn't manage to connect via phone, it always felt weird.

In the months that followed, every time we'd meet at the house or at Mom's place for dinner, there was a lot to catch up on. Things were changing quickly and dramatically for me, and I kept my brother up to date about how much money I was making and the new gigs I was taking on. At one point, I came home after a weekend of shows in Mississauga, and I dropped twenty thousand dollars in cash on his dresser.

I asked him, "Would you hang on to this for me?"

He looked at the stacks of cash and asked, "What am I supposed to do with it?"

I told him to just hang on to it. He kept staring at this pile of money on his bedroom dresser. "Just use it," I told him. That was my way of trying to pay him back for all the years he'd carried the mortgage and all the money he'd spent to help Mom and Dad. I was happy to be able to give something back.

It had been a year since Dad passed and just over a year since my *Comedy Now!* special had aired. YouTube had launched in February of that same year and someone—I don't even know who—uploaded my special onto it. I didn't upload it—I didn't even know how. I had gone viral and wish I could take credit for it.

At first, I was pissed that it had been put on the Web. In my mind, I was going, *Holy shit, my whole act is out there! This is crazy. I don't have a new act to take on the road.* Little did I know that the upload of the *Comedy Now!* special was my tipping point, my shot heard round the world.

I had taped that special in August of 2003 at the Masonic Temple on Yonge Street at Davenport, the same building where I first saw Run-D.M.C. and met them backstage, as well as the first place that I'd seen Public Enemy. This was the special where I'm wearing a white shirt, with the orangey background, the special where I first used my "Somebody Gonna Get a-Hurt Real Bad" and "Be a Man" routines.

Here's the backstory on the BE A MAN bit. It was never actually part of my original act. I just had no ending to that joke with the Chinese guy in the store, and I ended up throwing that line in. The really ironic part about that special was that "Be a Man" then became a catchphrase that people quoted all over the place. Now we sell T-shirts with "Be a Man" on them. Who knew?

After I finished taping that show, I went downstairs and all my friends were there: Jean Paul, my brother, Gavin Stephens and a bunch of other guys. They were all going "That was incredible!" and "That was a Gemini performance!" I was like," "Really?" I didn't know it was good. I thought it was okay.

After the special hit YouTube, I started getting more and more gigs and making more and more money—more than I could have ever imagined. I was also starting to get interest from the U.S., and I began making forays into different American universities, like Georgetown and Harvard and Rutgers. My brother was watching from the sidelines and guiding me. He decided he wanted a closer look at what was going on, so he came to Washington with me to see how things were being run by my then agent, Ed Smeall. Ed was a good guy who had broken away from Yuk Yuk's. He worked from home and knew the business very well, and accepted every gig.

Since I was new to this circuit, I didn't know there was any other way. Of course, as soon as my brother came down there with me and surveyed the scene, his business mind got to work. He has always had the ability to see beyond the present into the potential for the future, and when he saw how my gigs were run, he noticed some problems. One thing I remember he really didn't like was that I'd do a gig for one promoter in an area, and then my agent would accept a similar gig in the region with another promoter. My brother kept saying, "Hang on a sec. You just did a show with that promoter who

And here I was, an unknown Indian kid from Canada, coming to Harlem to do my set in front of what is traditionally an all-black audience.

came through for you. Now you're going to throw your loyalty to him out the window?" He also didn't like the fact that I never saw my contracts. There were other issues with those early gigs, too. There was no security at the venues, and people in the audience kept trying to record the shows. I'd be part of a whole night of entertainment that was often unstructured. Sometimes these universities would stage variety shows, with me and *bhangra* dancers and local kids who thought they were comedians and would promptly get booed off stage. It was all a bit of a mess.

These were the kinds of problems I'd hoped my manager would deal with so that I could concentrate on being funny on stage. As I talked with my brother, we realized a strategy was required, with rules and guidelines the various promoters would have to follow if I were to take on a gig. I was past the point of the amateur free-for-alls, and I knew that we could do better shows.

I had a chance to prove it soon afterward when I was booked for my first gig at the Apollo Theater in Harlem in April 2005. This was a pretty exciting opportunity. I'd never played a venue this prestigious before. In fact, no South Asian had ever headlined that venue. I'd heard so much over the years about the black audiences there who'd boo you off in seconds if they didn't like your act. And here I was, an unknown Indian kid from Canada, coming to Harlem to do my set in front of what is traditionally an all-black audience. Who was going to know who the hell I was? Every performer that's worth anything has performed there—Al Green, James Brown, Michael Jackson. I was going to perform on the same stage as

them? And who was going to show up in that room? Still, the gig was too cool to refuse, so I took it.

My brother and I stayed at the Waldorf-Astoria, and when it came time to leave for the theatre, our car didn't show. My brother, not yet my manager, got on the phone with the girl we thought was the promoter and screamed at her about me not having a car. (It turned out that she was a front for a promoter and fledgling comedian who was too scared to tell us that he was the promoter in case the show was a flop. This guy had no balls.) I still managed to get there early so that I could absorb the atmosphere of the building, so it wouldn't intimidate me. Everything fell into place that night. The audience was great; they were right there with me. I had a great set—I was freestyling like crazy. I could have just kept on going that night. It felt great. The people who work in that building were fantastic to me. They had never seen an Indian comic and they had never seen that crowd come in there. The audience was mostly South Asian and Asian, with a few black people here and there and a few white faces too. I even ended up making friends with some of the guys who worked there.

June 22, 2005.

I was on a real high after that show, and my brother and I now got serious about the possibility of him working for me. Basically, he said, "Listen, I hate my job, and I'm going to be quitting one way or another. Even if I make forty grand a year working with you, I'm going to be happier than doing what I'm doing."

I said, "Yeah. We should do that. Why don't you be my assistant?" That didn't go over so well. There was no way in hell my brother was going to be my assistant. He offered a counterproposal: he would be my manager.

In April 2005, he got his bonus cheque on a Friday and resigned the following Monday. He went out in style, and it gave both of us great pleasure to see him out of that nine-to-five corporate grind. Next, my brother put all his energy into building a strategy for my future, and over the course of the next year, under his stewardship and Dad's invisible-guardian hand, things exploded.

In June of 2005, we found ourselves in Los Angeles, setting up shows at both Royce Hall on the UCLA campus and at the world-famous Laugh Factory on Sunset Boulevard. Working with my brother, we had put together a strategy that would allow my performances at those two venues to be seen by as many industry VIPs and agents as possible. Both shows were completely sold out. It was really something. All of these kids who had only seen me on the Web were coming out in full force and showing me love.

Things were looking good. It was during that time that we also set up agency meetings. I needed representation in Los Angeles, and many of the big agencies had come out to see the shows. I didn't think too much at that time about getting the meetings. I now know how difficult it is to get the meetings that we got.

Interestingly, when we were taking meetings, there was one group that was never really on my radar: Creative Artists Agency. When they called to set up a meeting with me, my Canadian agent, Dani De Lio, who was down there with us, actually told them we didn't have any more openings in the schedule and that I wasn't really thinking of them. They were pretty stunned and refused to take no for an answer. They insisted, "You gotta come in and see us. We're CAA!" I mean, what could I say to that? So in I went.

The funny thing about agency meetings is that every office boardroom looks just like the next one. And the people in those boardrooms tend to look the same, too. There are all these guys wearing suits, waving their hands around and talking about what a great "brand" you could be, or how they'll have great "synergy" with you. All of this talk was going in one ear and out the other. Some of these meetings were pretty wacky. I got a sense that maybe some of those people were feeling a little too excited about me. In some instances, I sat there with all these talking heads, and I actually didn't get to say a single word. I was spoken at the whole time. It was all very, very surreal, and I wasn't used to being treated like "the next big thing."

When I went to CAA, I had already pretty much decided to sign on with The Gersh Agency. A couple of guys from Gersh had come to my shows and I liked them, as well as Bob Gersh, who actually hosted a meeting with me at his home in Beverly Hills. Bob was a good guy. After the group presentation at CAA—which was the usual "We'll get you on *Oprah*," "We'll get you on Letterman, no problem," "And you should be meeting with so and so"—we were met by Rob Light. Rob is one of the partners at CAA, so this was kind of a big deal. All the agents in the conference room were wearing suits and ties, but Rob was wearing jeans and sneakers. He took me around to his office and was telling me about all the other clients the firm represents—Brad Pitt, Tom Cruise, George Clooney. You name the A-list star, and chances are they're with CAA. Still, none of that meant anything to me. But as I sat in Rob's office, I noticed KISS posters on his walls. It turns out that CAA represents KISS.

All of a sudden, I was a twelve-year-old boy again, and I had the opportunity to be represented by the same agents who represented my boyhood heroes. To take things even further, Rob proceeded to get lead singer Paul Stanley on speakerphone. I was over the moon.

I was talking with KISS! That was it: this was where I was going to sign. I was going to be represented by the same agency that represents KISS! Maybe this was not the best strategy for choosing an agent, but there are certain things that stick with you from when you're a kid that you just can't shake. It's now been five years since I signed with CAA, and I have to say that there are some really good people there who have done some fantastic things for me. They know who they are, and so do I.

Gene smiled and said, "Can I get you something to drink as well?"

Right after I joined the CAA roster, Rob saw to it that Gene Simmons himself came out to my show at the Laugh Factory. He brought a fellow Canadian, actress Shannon Tweed, with him—I knew her, of course, from *Falcon Crest* . . . and from *Playboy*. Both Gene and Shannon are insanely nice, extremely tall and larger than life. I was pretty blown away when I looked out into the audience and saw one of my heroes looking back at me and laughing at my jokes. I got to meet Gene after the show and talk to him for a while. Fans were coming up to me and wanting to take pictures. One of them turned around and handed her camera to Gene and said, "Hey man, can you snap a picture of Russell and me?" So Gene obliges, then the girl says, "Can you turn the camera sideways and take another one?" Gene smiled and said, "Can I get you something

Gene Simmons, me and Shannon Tweed.

to drink as well?" So there I am, having my picture taken with a fan . . . and Gene Simmons is the one taking the picture! Really, it was like the world had turned upside down. At some point during all the madness, Gene looked at me and said, "You know what? If you were a girl, I'd fuck you." That was probably the first—and the last—time in my life when I was glad to have a dude say something like that to me.

Now that things were really taking off and my brother was manning the ship, he started to focus on what he calls "data mining"—rebuilding my website and making sure we had a solid database through which to communicate to you guys, the fans. Whenever something important is going on with me or I've got a show in your city, I send you an email blast so you know what's up. I do use Facebook and MySpace and Twitter (well, who uses MySpace anymore?), but I'm not really one of those social-networky, blog-happy guys. I'm not about to bother you every day to tell you what colour socks I'm wearing. (Although I should mention that I do like to wear colourful socks. It's my thing.) From what I can see, most of you respect the fact that I don't harass you. And here's something else: I actually hate talking about myself, so I'm not about to send you emails going on and on about me. Doing this book has been a challenge, because to sit here and just talk about myself seems ridiculous. Anything that I say sounds like I'm bragging, and I hate when people do that . . . speaking of which. . . .

So now that I had a fan base set up, the next thing we decided to do was shoot a special and get a DVD out there. My brother worked tirelessly behind the scenes to get everything right, but I'll tell you it wasn't easy. Several companies were interested in producing the special and distributing the DVD, but their visions didn't necessarily jive with what my brother and I wanted do. The way we saw things, we owed my fans a really good product because they'd supported me and had helped me get to this level. We felt that by offering them a wicked DVD, with lots of good bonus features and audio commentary, we would be honouring their part in the whole process. We didn't want to skimp, and we wanted to offer some added value for fans who couldn't make it to see me live. Now, producers don't usually think that way, and Brother and I started to wonder if it wouldn't be better to produce and finance things ourselves. Brother's the type who would do anything to see things done right. We had already turned down Comedy Central, who wanted me to do a half-hour special instead of an hour-long show. My agent, Nick Nuciforo, said that we shouldn't do a half-hour, considering the amount of material that I had at my disposal. Then Comedy Central came back and asked if I'd tape my special at their inaugural Miami Comedy Festival. At the time, I didn't think that Miami would be the best place for me to do it. We were pushing to produce this special ourselves, but the agents thought we were crazy. We even had CAA check with Comedy Central to see if they'd buy a Russell Peters special through acquisitions. They replied that we'd turned them down twice now, so "No!"

In the end, we made a deal with Parallel Entertainment, a management and production company that had a "put-through" arrangement with Comedy Central (a deal where Comedy Central had to broadcast any specials that Parallel gave them). Parallel also had a DVD distribution deal with Warner Music in the States.

Working with all these outside entities was new to us. We'd grown used to doing our own thing and planning our shows in Canada. All of a sudden, we had new agents telling us how to do things and when to do them. We had a big production company deciding where we'd record and a broadcaster telling us when they'd take delivery of "the product."

It was decided that we'd shoot at the Warfield Theatre in San Francisco and that I'd do two shows back to back in one night. It was a nightmare. I had a cold at the time and my throat was shot, but the show had to go on. Ideally, it would have been better for me to shoot about three months later, when I was feeling better and had a chance

At some point, a girl in this group actually puked—I'm talking projectile vomit.

to fine-tune the material more. But when you've got a crew of more than a hundred people working on the production and fans have put down cash for their tickets, the show must go on.

The first show was fantastic. It went really well, and the audience was great. When the second show started, I knew we were in trouble. A whole crew of Indian kids arrived in the third row. At first, I was happy to see the browns in the crowd, but then, as I continued the set, I realized they were drunk out of their minds. They started yelling things out at me at the top of their lungs, and they weren't even making any sense. They were yelling old bits, like "Be a Man" and "Do Somebody!" I was getting increasingly pissed off. At some point, a girl in this group actually puked—I'm talking projectile vomit here—right in the middle of me recording my first major special with an American broadcaster. The next thing I knew, her friend came over to help her and wiped out in the girl's puke. Great. I'm trying my best to go on with the show and give what should be the best performance of my life, but it's becoming impossible. At some point, I just gave up and turned to the audience and said, "None of this is going to be usable." I was so fucking angry.

When it was all over, I was really concerned about how the whole thing was going to turn out, but after postproduction and the editing process, the special turned out well. You couldn't tell I was sick, and you couldn't spot any projectile vomit on the stage (the camera guys managed to cut around it). If you listen carefully, there's this one spot where I do my Chinese joke, and you can hear my voice crack just a bit, but overall, the material worked, and people really like it. We wanted to add more bonus features to the DVD, but the producers didn't feel it was necessary and didn't okay the cost. There was also drama over the cover art. I didn't like what they had come up with, and we were frantically searching for an alternative that we could all agree upon. It got so bad that at one point, when we were on tour in Australia, my brother was on the phone with Warners and the producers and they even discussed selling everything back to us. In the end, it all worked out. Mind you, that didn't stop one of the executive producers from bad-mouthing me and my brother around town, saying that we were difficult to work with. I don't think we were difficult; we just had a different vision for the project than he did and weren't doing the whole "yes sir, no sir" thing with these guys. We stood our ground when we needed to, and they weren't expecting it—especially from a couple of guys who were not only Canadian, but Indian too, double-outsiders who in their minds should have just been happy to be there. My brother had already been through that mentality at his corporate gig and wasn't having it. All in all, a good first lesson on some of the things we would come to expect from Hollywood.

Once the DVD of *Outsourced* came out, and after the special was broadcast on Comedy Central on August 29, 2006, sure enough, some downloading bastard posted it on YouTube. Once again, the world was picking up on what I was doing, and once again, I had nothing to do with it. Like I said before, I don't like talking about myself, so when *Outsourced* was released, I had to do a whole whack of press . . . and this was, and still is, a challenge for me. The record label in the States had set up a series of radio morning-show call-ins for me to promote it. These radio tours always suck unless the morning guys know who you are, and at that time, 99.9 per cent of them had no idea who I was.

Once I got back to Toronto, it was another round of press. Newspapers, radio and television. I hated doing all that press and it shows if you read the interviews. My brother spazzed out on me over the phone when I missed a phone interview with a Toronto paper and I said some not-so-nice things about "all these managers and agents with their hands in my pocket." Unfortunately, I'm not very good at hiding my feelings. I couldn't go from being yelled at by my brother—

who was just frustrated in general about trying to get me to do press—to being Happy Guy in the next interview.

I should point out that by this point, the fall of 2006, my entire world had changed radically. I had all these agents and people in Hollywood telling me that I was the next big thing and how great I was. I had also made more money in the preceding twelve months than I had in my entire career. It was a lot to handle, and I didn't handle it very well. I didn't start drinking or doing drugs like some guys do, but I was definitely adjusting to the challenges of growing fame and the mounting demands that celebrity puts on you. Let me be clear: I was still the same guy I was two years earlier, but everyone else was starting to treat me differently, including my own friends.

I had a new million-dollar home in Los Angeles, new cars, new friends, basically a whole new lifestyle. My brother was quick to tell me that I had to make compromises with my time and that I had to promote myself more if I wanted to maintain that new lifestyle. I got to the point where I was saying crazy things like "I don't care about playing bigger venues! I'll just go back to playing clubs. I don't want to do press or talk about myself. I'll just walk away from all of it! I don't care about the money!" Even though I had dreamed about getting to that place for the better part of my life, I wasn't prepared when it actually happened.

All of this put a lot of stress on my brother and me. There was even a time when we stopped talking for a while and he seriously thought about not managing me anymore. He was going through his own changes too. He'd bought a new home in Oakville and had recently gotten engaged. We weren't just a couple of close brothers who lived in a small townhouse in Woodbridge anymore. And what was going to happen with my new DVD? Would anyone even buy it? Was it any good? My world had grown so big so fast, and I needed to grow as well.

The fall of 2006 was difficult. After *Outsourced* came out in Canada in September, I had a bunch of tour dates set up. Now that it was out on DVD and everyone would know my act, what the fuck was I supposed to do when I got on stage? As far as I was concerned, I had no fresh material! My brother kept insisting that I could do the material from *Outsourced*. "It's not like people have it memorized," he told me. As far as I'm concerned, once I release material, it's done for me. I wipe it from my memory bank and need to start over with new stuff.

I remember one show I did in Brampton, at the Rose Theatre. It's a small theatre and they made me a special offer as part of their grand opening. The tension between my brother and me was high, and I showed up for the show right at the last minute, still convinced that I had nothing to offer the crowd. I did the show . . . and freestyled most of it. I included lots of local references about my hometown, and the crowd seemed happy. I wasn't, though. I left for gigs in Ottawa a day or so later—without my brother. He thought it would be better for him not to be there. I did the shows in Ottawa, and again, rather than draw from my existing repertoire, I freestyled a lot of the show. It wasn't great, and a couple of fans later wrote to complain. What can I say? I just couldn't bear repeating myself, and in my own way I was trying to give the fans something new.

After Ottawa, I went back to L.A. and was completely depressed. My brother and I were hardly talking, except through very brief emails. On September 19, after receiving a list of "pending" items from him—tours in Singapore and India, media opportunities—I finally emailed him back about how depressed I was: "I don't feel like talking to anyone. I feel blah and lethargic. No thoughts, no motivation. I'm uninspired and down. I want to go to sleep for a long time and wake up in the future . . ." At 3:38 A.M., my brother wrote back: "The most important thing to me is that you're happy. If you're not happy, I'm not happy." (This was thirty-six years deep and had nothing to do with him being my manager.) "You're overanalyzing everything and putting too much pressure on yourself . . . . It's always been my job and will always be my job to make sure that you're okay

I finally emailed him back about how depressed I was: "I don't feel like talking to anyone. I feel blah and lethargic."

and to guide you—whether you're the biggest comedian in the world or the funniest guy working in a factory. Frankly, it's the only thing I've ever been good at." He also talked about his own battles with depression, which I didn't know anything about. Through this email exchange, we effectively closed off this dark chapter and started to move forward with our plans for 2007.

My brother was right by my side during all the madness that came after that, and he's at my side to this day (even writing these words right now)—managing all aspects of what has become a very well-oiled machine. I think what we have, both as brothers and as professionals, is a special thing. Often, we'll meet people who will say, "Oh, I wish I could work with my brother the way you two work together,

Skinny '90s brothers.

Baghdad, November 2007.

but he and I don't get along." I don't really respond to these comments, but in my head I'm always thinking, *How can you not get along with your brother? He's your brother!* And I guess that makes us different from a lot of other people out there. Family matters in a way that I'm not sure it does for everyone. There's no question in my mind that my brother and I are in this together. We've always had a very close and unified relationship, and if you don't have that, nothing else seems worth the trouble.

On our way to Australia, 2006.

Backstage in San Fran for Outsourced.

North Peel Secondary School
Graduation
Dinner Dance
Aboard the "The Empire Sandy"
Friday the Twenty-fourth of June
nineteen hundred and eighty eight
at Seven fifteen in the evening
Admission $30.00 per person
(Non-Refundable)
Dress-Semi Formal

PART TWO

MADE IN BRAMPTON

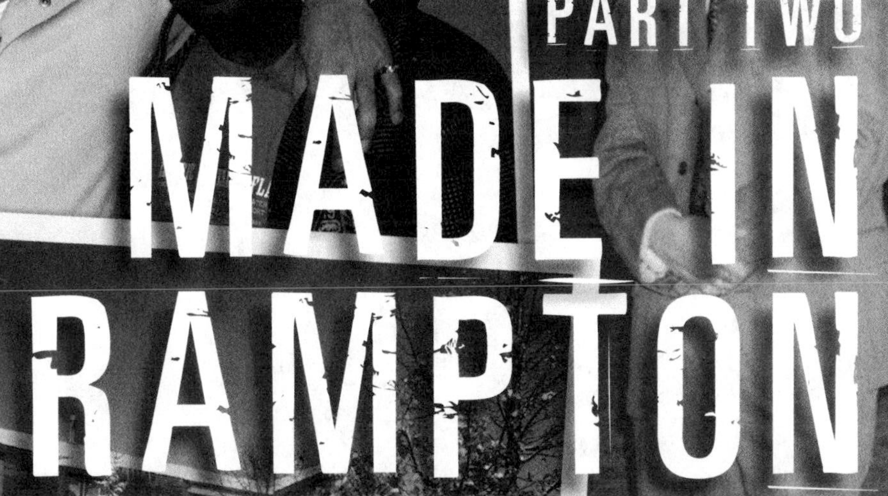

AFTER TENTH GRADE, I GOT KICKED OUT OF "REGULAR" HIGH SCHOOL—

"regular" high school being where most of you went to school. *I* got kicked out.

I don't know how it works in America, but in Canada, in high school you earn eight credits every year, so by the end of tenth grade, you should have sixteen credits. Well . . . I had seven. Actually, I had five—but I picked up two in summer school because I was trying to catch up.

So the school I was going to genuinely thought I was slow. Like they thought I was a fucking retard. They just did. You know how I knew they thought I was slow? Not because they kicked me out and sent me to the "retard school"—that was obvious.

I knew they thought I was slow because I remember the day the guidance counsellor called me to the office. He started speaking to me all *sloooow*. Now, at the time I didn't know that *he* thought I was slow. I thought *he* was slow—and I didn't want to make him feel bad, what with all my "fast speech."

CHAPTER 5

I LIKE TO . . . COOK?

BACK IN THE MID-'70S, when I was in grade school, no one was really aware of ADD—attention deficit disorder, or ADHD as it's often called now. In case you've been living in a hole and have no idea what this is, it's a disorder characterized by inattention, hyperactivity and impulsive behaviour, and it's not something you just grow out of. I have never been officially diagnosed, but it's obvious to anyone who knows me well that my powers of concentration are scattered all over the place. You may have even noticed in this book that I jump around a lot. It's just the way my mind works. I'm always doing several things at the same time. It's not uncommon for me to be talking to someone, listening to music, checking my iPhone and working out a comedy segment in my head, all at the same time. ADD follows you throughout your life, but if you're lucky, you learn to get better at managing it. It's pretty common today for kids to be diagnosed with attention problems, but when I was growing up no one really knew what the hell these were, and kids who were like me were often dismissed as dumb, lazy or troubled.

Throughout school, I put up with years of the same kind of comments on my report cards from teachers at Georges Vanier Catholic School, where I spent nine years of my elementary life. My teachers would make comments like "Russell is sharp but fails to apply himself." In other words, they knew I wasn't an idiot, but they suspected I might be a lazy ass. For the record, I'm *not* an idiot but I *am* a lazy ass. My parents never seemed overly concerned about my crazy energy levels and lack of attention. As far as they were concerned, I was just a kid. And you know, I'm lucky that I had friends at the time who didn't see me as a fuckup but as just another kid who wanted to goof around like they did. One of my best friends, Marlon Dubeau, had ADD too.

Marlon's the closest thing I have to a second brother. We met at one of the parks behind the townhouses on Bramalea Road when I was eight and he was seven. He was this little Jamaican kid, and when other kids were picking on me, he wasn't. He was like, "Hey, why don't you come to my house and we'll eat crackers?" So we went to his house, opened a can of tuna and brought out some Ritz crackers and Kool-Aid to eat on his front steps. That was the sweetest, most delicious Kool-Aid I've ever tasted in my life . . . because Marlon put so much friggin' sugar in it.

Elementary school was pretty good for me—for the most part. Still, this was where I started to get a sense that there might be something just a little different about me, something that set me apart in ways I didn't quite understand at the time. I'd show up in the schoolyard, and the other kids would say, "Ooo, the Paki's here." I'd be like, "Where? Where's the Paki?" For a long time, I didn't get it. I thought the Paki was some sort of ghost or something, and when the kids would yell, "Run, run! The Paki's here!" I'd high-tail it out of there along with them.

"Run, run! The Paki's here!"

So things like that happened on occasion, but still, elementary school was good. By Grade 8, I had a clique of friends, and in the summer before I began Grade 9—the summer of '84—my crew and I spent almost every day breakdancing. Rap and hip-hop were just emerging. I felt like that music defined me, like it was my discovery. We were listening to "Freakazoid" by Midnight Star, "Rockit" by Herbie Hancock and "It's Nasty" by Grandmaster Flash and the Furious Five. We'd learn our moves by watching videos, like Malcolm McLaren's "Buffalo Gals," "Party Train" by the Gap Band and "Save the Overtime for Me" by Gladys Knight & the Pips. That's all we ever wanted to do, just breakdance all the time. Mom and Dad's front lawn on Finchgate was totally dead because I'd covered it with cardboard for the entire summer. We would practise routines all day. We would time them for just when we saw the bus coming down Balmoral Drive. It would stop right in front of our house and we'd do the routine for the people on the bus.

All the guys had their best move, and mine was a shuffle. I'd start on my knees and then spin around really fast, all the while smashing my one knee against the ground. One day, my knees really swelled up and I thought, *I can't do that anymore*. Another time, I was practising in the gym at Georges Vanier, and I was doing a stand-up dive. I would stand up and just dive straight to the ground and go into the worm. I was really good at it—until one day I hit wrong and my legs bent over me. For about a minute, I thought I was paralyzed. I have never felt that kind of pain in my life.

That summer of '84 was the best of my life. I was breakdancing and I was cool and I was meeting chicks for the first time. I had no idea how miserable I was about to become once September arrived and I found myself at Chinguacousy Secondary School, a.k.a. Ching, in Brampton. The transition did not go well. I was the smallest kid in the class—like crazy small and scrawny—and, of course, I was brown. A lot of people may think I had problems just because I was Indian. That was *a* problem, but it wasn't *the* problem. My size made me an easy target for the bullies, who then threw in a touch of racism to top it off. I was easy to pick on and had kind of an outgoing personality. And definitely, I had kind of a smart mouth. Guys would say something to me and I'd say something back, and that didn't make the situation any better. I would talk back just to be clever or funny, and these guys weren't clever or funny. What they were was violent.

I remember walking home and just bawling my ass off, pretty much every day, actually. I got called a Paki all the fucking time.

When I arrived as a "minor niner" in Ching's halls, the bullying increased to the point where I was punched in the head, spit on and even kicked in the stomach with Kodiak boots. I remember leaving Ching crying a lot—not that I'd let people see me crying, but I remember walking home and just bawling my ass off, pretty much every day, actually. I got called a Paki all the fucking time. A couple of times I would start making friends with a girl and then, as we walked home,

I might be holding her hand or even kissing her, and then one of her friends would see us and say something to her like "What are you doing with that fucking Paki?" That would be the end of things between us.

One afternoon, I was right by the water fountain close to the library when these five black guys picked me up, really high, and they were going to put me into a garbage can head first. That incident wasn't racially motivated; it was just straight-up bullying. They were holding me up, and then somebody yelled, "Principal's coming!" and they just dropped me onto the ground, right on my back—*bam*. I got up and went crazy and started swinging the garbage can at them. They were laughing and just sort of scattered away.

I still remember all the times I would come home from school in Grade 9 and tell my parents, "That guy called me a Paki again today." And my dad would ask, "What's this kid's last name?"

"Jankowski," I said.

"So he's Polish . . . You go back to school tomorrow, and you go up to that boy and you tell him he's a Polack and that Polacks do this, that and the other. That's what you do. And if that doesn't work, you punch him right in the mouth."

And I'd say to my dad, "Yeah. Okay . . ."

My dad always recommended words before weapons, and that's what he was trying to get at here—not that he never resorted to violence. Believe me, he did. Dad would tell me stories about when he was a kid in boarding school. Some classmate was teasing him in front of a bunch of people and my dad was embarrassed. He waited, and then one day, when the bully was the only one left in the shower—it was a communal shower—he marched in there with this little club (a miniature pine baseball bat about twelve to eighteen inches long) and smashed the guy across the face with it. He broke the kid's nose. Then he turned around and left. The bully never said a word to him again. My dad took that little club with him to Canada in the '60s. I remember seeing that thing my whole life. He used to keep it right beside his bed when he was sleeping in case somebody broke into the house.

The bottom line is that my dad was a genuine, old-school tough guy. He had that in him. It wasn't like he was faking it or it was machismo. It wasn't like it was second nature for him, either. If he was going to let that side of him out, he'd think long and hard beforehand. And when I was a kid, he was encouraging me to be the same way: to devise a plan to protect myself, and then to carry it through.

I never ended up following his advice, though. The problem was I just wasn't a confrontational kid. Even now, as an adult, I'm actually not that confrontational. As a kid, I did appreciate my dad's outrage and his efforts to help me deal with the bullies myself. The truth of the matter is that what I was dealing with was pure ignorance, ignorance at the most basic level, and you can't use logic against an ignoramus. It just doesn't work.

I also never wanted my father to be involved because, deep down, part of me felt like we really were second-class citizens. I always felt that I was prey and that my dad was prey, too. I was scared that if we did something about the bullying, if we brought it to the authorities—say the police, for instance—they would take the side of the perpetrator. I didn't want to put my parents through that, especially not my dad, so I just put up with a lot of nasty shit. I knew it wasn't fair; I knew it wasn't right. But I also knew that you can't fight fire with fire. You have to find a different way.

Things at Ching were getting pretty bad through Grade 9; the only fun I had was out of school. I was very, very unhappy there. Looking back, I could almost say I was depressed. I didn't have any friends in school; they were all at other schools and I felt totally alone. I was having troubles getting my credits. I got 13 per cent in typing in Grade 9. I was never a studious guy. Mom used to beg me to pass my courses. She'd say, "Just get 50 per cent. Just don't fail." And I would try . . . but I would still fail. Something inside of me just told me that everything they were teaching me was completely irrelevant. It meant nothing to me. And the teachers . . . A good teacher knows how to teach everybody. But at Ching, it was all just reciting, and focusing on the kids who were already getting it, instead of helping those who weren't, like me. That's something I really hate, and now in my comedy, I make sure that people, normal people, are going to get my jokes. I want everyone, even the guy at the back of the room, to be in on the joke with me and not to feel left out.

I want everyone, even the guy at the back of the room, to be in on the joke with me and not to feel left out.

By Grade 10, right near the end of the year, a guidance counsellor, Mr. Flannery, called me into his office. He started speaking to me *reeeee-eeallly slooooooowly*. He said, "What do you like to *do*? Is there anything you *like*, Russell?" He was literally talking to me as if something wasn't clicking in my head. I was thinking, *What's wrong with this guy? What do you want from me, dude?* I was fifteen years old and I didn't know what I wanted to do with the rest of my life, so I just answered, "I don't know." And then I think I told him I liked to . . . cook? And he went, "Oh, *really*? Let me take you on a tour of North Peel and show you what they can offer you." North Peel is a trade school that all the kids in the 'hood referred to as the "school for retards."

That's how I ended up at North Peel—because a guidance counsellor at Chinguacousy thought I was *slooooow*. North Peel had a reputation as a tough school, and I was already sick of getting my ass whooped by a bunch of losers. The time had come for me to defend myself. So, in September of '86, I took up boxing. My good friend Willie was an incredible boxer. He was the most elusive fighter you've ever seen in your life. He was practically impossible to hit. If Willie had stayed focused on fighting and hadn't been so punch drunk at such a young age, he could've really been somebody big. I had known Willie since early elementary school, and we had been in high school together at Ching. Dad convinced me to go to the gym with Willie, so I did. It was Champion Gym, owned and run by John Melich, right behind the Latin Quarter on Melanie Drive in Brampton. Willie and I were the youngest guys at the gym, and there we were learning to box with John, Dwight Fraser and Rick Souce. Dwight and Rick were the big dogs in the gym. They were pros. Dwight actually fought in the '84 Olympics.

When I first started boxing, I didn't even know how to throw a punch. It took me a good few weeks—if not months—just to learn how to throw a left jab. John wouldn't let us use our right hands at all. I just worked my left hand, did a lot of shadowboxing, skipping and hitting the bags. And once I kind of got the rhythm with my left hand, maybe about five months later, I went into the ring for the first time to spar with Willie, who was an incredible fighter. When Willie and I sparred for the first time, it was also the first time they'd put sparring gloves on me; they were so heavy—they weighed about a pound each—and I was such a small kid. As soon as I went to throw a punch, my arm just dropped straight down. So I was in the ring with Willie and couldn't hit him for the life of me. He'd been boxing his whole life. He was avoiding punches, and I'd miss him literally by a millimetre. He would move just enough not to get hit. His footwork, his upper-body work, were incredible. Fortunately for me, Willie was actually a very gentle guy, and when he punched me, he'd go really light. Maybe that's why he never pursued boxing professionally, because he never had that killer instinct. Inside and outside of the ring, he was just a good human being.

Marlon had also started training at the gym with us. He was having a lot of trouble with his left jab. He couldn't quite coordinate it properly, so John Melich made Marlon put his right arm behind his back and spar with this guy Ramon. Because Marlon was fighting with only the one hand, Ramon kept landing punches on him. He just kept hitting him and hitting him. Marlon was getting angrier and angrier, until he unleashed this massive right arm and knocked Ramon across the ring, where he collapsed in the corner and started bawling. Marlon has the most incredible strength you've ever seen.

Willie's uncle, Gary Blackburn, was at the gym with us and started training us too. We would go to the matches that Melich would promote and Dwight and Rick would fight in. I was in the gym pretty much constantly and was progressing well. Melich liked my jab. He liked the way I punched and moved, and one day he said to me, "Kid, I'm gonna get you a fight in a couple of weeks." I didn't want to fight. I definitely didn't want to become a pro boxer. I just wanted to learn how to defend myself. So when Melich said that, I stopped going to the gym for the next three weeks. When I eventually showed up again, he said, "What happened to you? You embarrassed me." I made up some excuse about being busy. John tried again to put me in the ring as an amateur, and I didn't show up again. After a while, he got the hint.

In total, I went to that gym for about three or four years—every Monday, Wednesday and Thursday for three hours. In the '90s, I stopped. I had gotten everything I wanted out of boxing and didn't want to do it professionally. I would go back every now and then and the guys there would treat me like I had never left and work me really hard. I'd be like, "Jesus, guys, I haven't been here in six months. Give me a break." One time I had to spar with this giant Jamaican guy who was a heavyweight—225 pounds, strong as an ox and dumb as shit. At the time, I probably weighed about 150 pounds. Melich said, "Russell, this guy's sparring partner didn't show up, so do you want to go in the ring?"

I said, "No."

"Don't worry. He's just working on his defence." When a guy's working on defence, you're supposed to hit him and he's supposed to just move out of the way without hitting you back.

I asked, "Are you sure?" and Melich said, "Yeah, just defence." So I went in the ring and started hitting the guy. Me and my big mouth started talking shit to him, saying things like, "Man, you suck! Look at me! I'm not even good and I'm hitting you." I was talking all kinds of shit, and then the guy saw an opening and gave me a body shot. It dropped me immediately.

So, that's how I learned to fight, and that's how I learned to protect myself at North Peel—so I wouldn't be bullied there the way

I had been at Ching. People can say what they want about North Peel, but it was the best thing that ever happened to me. People there treated me like an equal, and there was no racism. It was a much blacker school, but these kids weren't trying to fit in with the white guys and the jocks. These were real 'hood kids—hardened, bad-ass kids. But I fared a lot better with the bad-asses than with the bullies. The major difference between bullies and bad-asses, as I was about to learn, is that bullies are all bark and no bite. They'll pick on you only if they think they can, but if there's a chance of them actually getting hurt, they back off really fast. Bad-asses, on the other hand, will never do that. If they know they can beat you, they'll beat you. Bad-asses don't even bother picking on you, but if you mess with them, you're in big trouble.

I learned these distinctions early on at North Peel Secondary School. Consequently, I got in only two fights there. The first time, this guy kept calling me a fag. Every time I passed him in the hallway, he said it again. Finally, it was just me and him in the hallway, and after warning him to stop, he said the word one more time. "What did you say?" I asked, and I pushed him against the locker—boom, boom. I hit him, two left hooks in the ribs . . . and I cracked them. His mom came to the school the next day to complain about what I'd done to her son.

The second fight was with this Croatian kid, a big dude who kept mocking me about this girl who had dumped me. I really liked her. She was the prettiest girl in the school. I was already feeling crappy about losing the girl, and then this guy had to rub it in. Everybody was standing at the foot of the stairwell and he said he knew tae kwon do or something, and I said, "Shut the fuck up!" and started punching him, but not very hard. He started laughing then, and I got really mad. In my head I was thinking, *You have to do something now or he's gonna kick your ass.*

So I grabbed him by his shirt, and I heard it rip. I don't know where I got the strength, but the next thing I knew, I had lifted him up and thrown him across the stairwell. His legs hit the railing and his head hit the wall. He was lying there on the floor, stunned, and then he said, “What’s your problem, man?” I yelled back the corniest thing—“That’s what happens when you fuck with me!”—and continued up the stairs past him like an idiot. That’s pretty much how I transformed from being bullied to becoming one of the so-called bad-asses, and from that time on, I had a much easier time of things in school.

I only do jokes about stuff I really care about.

But here’s something weird: whenever I got into fights, my ass would twitch. My ass cheek would literally start jumping the same way some guys can move their pecs. My butt cheek would just go nuts. It was a bizarre nervous thing. To this day, my butt starts to do that if I get nervous. Fortunately, I’m a bit more confident with my skills now, and at age forty, you really shouldn’t be fighting people anyhow. The only things I fight now are colds . . . and maybe arthritis.

It was at North Peel that I started to hang out with a whole bunch of other guys who had things in common with me. They were mostly of Caribbean descent and were mostly black, but we got along. They were teenagers, just like me, but kids who were maybe a little bit poorer than most. Some of my friends at that time were not necessarily broke, but they were not walking into a really nice house at the end of the day.

Apart from actually having a social life with kids who had my back, North Peel also saved my ass academically. It was there where teachers respected me and considered my potential for the first time, and they replaced some of my awkwardness with true confidence. That’s why I do jokes about North Peel to this day: I only do jokes about stuff I really care about.

There were two teachers at North Peel who rank among the most committed people I have ever met: Mr. Kolar and Ms. Kelly. Technically speaking, Ms. Kelly wasn’t even my teacher, but I would often skip my classes and go hang out in her sewing class just because she was the coolest woman in the world. Her class was one of the few places in the school where I could be who I was and do what I wanted . . . and it didn't hurt that her class was full of chicks. I'd walk in and just be myself and make them laugh. In some ways, Ms. Kelly's sewing class was one of my first audiences. I never learned to sew on a button, but it was nice to feel that for once a teacher actually liked the fact that I was hanging around.

And then there was my chef teacher, Fred Kolar, who inspired me to follow my dreams, even though at the time I didn't have a clue what those dreams were. I mean, how can you figure out your future when the adults around you say you can't focus, you're up to no good and you're really not going to get anywhere? But then there was Mr. Kolar, and he's one of these people who remind you that anyone can do a job, but it takes a special person—a real professional—to give it everything they've got. This was a man who chose to teach as a vocation, and let's face it, it's not like teachers are in it for the amazing paycheque.

Fred Kolar is a guy who goes above and beyond. Here's a guy who is a world-class chef, at one time the head of the Escoffier Society, and he decided that wasn't enough, that he wanted to help kids. In Fred's class, everyone was treated as an individual, no matter how messed up they were—and believe me, there were some pretty messed-up kids in our class. He was the first teacher I ever had who would swear at the students when we would screw up the food we were cooking. He'd be like, "What the fuck are you doing?" But he always did this in the right way, never to make you feel like shit. It was because he cared.

There was one time when we made pâté and he put me in charge. The pâté had liquor in it, and he had to be very careful when he pulled out liquor in class because it was supposed to go in the food, not down our throats. Mr. Kolar took me and a couple others to a food show at the Metro Toronto Convention Centre. One of the head chefs from the Four Seasons tasted the pâté I'd made and said it was one of the best he'd ever tasted. The guy started talking to Kolar because they knew each other, and then Kolar was like, "Russell, this guy wants to give you a job!"

"Really?"

"Yeah. When you're done high school, you should definitely look into it."

Obviously, I never did, but I was really flattered. It was the first time somebody said that I was good at something.

Mr. Kolar and me, backstage at the Air Canada Centre, 2007.

Above and beyond teaching us kids how to cook, Fred taught us about demeanour, about thinking about others and putting yourself in their shoes before you decide to act out or judge. That's a pretty incredible lesson to have passed along. To this day, I still keep in touch with Fred, a man who was an inspiration for me when I was a small, brown, mouthy teen, and who remains an inspiration and a friend to this day.

North Peel was a turning point in my life. That school gave me a sense of community and belonging. That isn't to say I was an angel during that time. I became the kind of guy who, if you needed something, anything, I'd be able to get it for you. If you needed a leather jacket, I knew somebody who worked at the mall who could get it for you. A stereo? I could get you one cheap. I was always the link between demand and supply.

This reputation and ability to get stuff ultimately led me to supplying drugs. I needed money, so I started selling small amounts of hash and weed to people I knew. To be honest, all I wanted was to make enough to go to Burger King and McDonald's when I felt like it. And I wasn't doing drugs myself; I wasn't some thug operating as part of a cartel, either. I was just a guy who knew where to get stuff and knew people who wanted it—mostly white-collar people who didn't want to risk pulling up at a corner somewhere to buy recreational drugs.

I wasn't a very good dealer. My supplier knew that I didn't do any drugs, so he could trust me to move small amounts on consignment. One day—actually my *first* day selling drugs—I picked up an ounce of black hash from him and took it back home. In the basement of my parents' house I chopped the ounce into dime pieces, wrapped them in tinfoil and went off to sell them. I sold a dime to the older brother of a friend. He took the hash, left, and thirty minutes later came back to see me.

I was the only drug dealer around with a return policy.

"I don't want it. Give me my money back," he demanded.

"Uhm . . . okay," I said. I was the only drug dealer around with a return policy.

So he handed the dime back to me and I gave him back his twenty bucks. He left, and I started to wonder about what he'd given me. I opened the foil and the hash looked the same, felt the same. Black hash is black on the outside and brown in the middle . . . but it didn't smell right. I broke the piece open and yes, it looked brown in the middle. Hmmm . . . I didn't know what it was supposed to taste like, but I touched the piece to my tongue anyway. It was sweet . . . kind of tasted like licorice—because it *was* licorice. Nibs. He had used the black hash, gotten a full refund and given me back a Nibs.

I ultimately stopped selling drugs because I wasn't making any real money off of it. There was nothing cool about selling and I was just taking a huge risk carrying drugs around with me. I was no Tony Montana and I knew it, so I quit.

Sometimes I think about how things could have turned out for me, how things could have gone differently. Marlon and I used to hang with this guy named Mike Boudreau. The three of us were tight. We even went to the prom together because none of us could get dates. Dad let me borrow his car, a burgundy Cutlass Ciera. Marlon had brought his ghetto blaster because Dad's car never had a cassette deck. After the prom, the three of us drove around Brampton, playing "Plug Tunin'" by De La Soul and "Small Time Hustler" by the Dismasters. We kept singing along with and rewinding that track over and over because it was so dope. We had a great time together.

A year or two after we graduated, Mike was dating this girl and they broke up. Then either she or her parents told him not to come around anymore. Mike wasn't having that. One night he broke into her parents' house and made his way to their bedroom. He proceeded to stab the father to death and then stabbed the girl's mother in the eye. He just went crazy. He then tried to kidnap his ex-girlfriend and ended up getting caught in Lexington, Kentucky.

There was another friend of ours, Richard Smith, a.k.a. Superman, who used to break into cars and steal stereos. One night, he was breaking into cars in Major Oaks Park at Highway 410 and Williams Parkway, which was a popular place to go "parking." He opened the door of one of the cars parked there to find a couple making out in the backseat. The guy in the car started freaking out and got into a fight with Rich. In the course of the scuffle, Richard ended up stabbing the guy and the guy died. Richard went to jail for murder.

Then there was Norman, a kid I knew from North Peel. He used to smoke a lot of weed. One day, he and his dad got into an argument. Norman beat his father to death, then propped him in a chair, sat down beside him in the living room and watched TV. When people say that weed doesn't mess you up, I say, "I beg to differ."

And then there was Peter Mann. Dad and I actually went to his house a few times to watch fights because he had a satellite dish and got HBO. Peter was a big boxing fan. I remember we watched Michael Nunn knock out Sumbu Kalambay in under two minutes in 1989. One day, he told me he was going to kill his ex-girlfriend. At the time, I thought he was talking shit. He went and stabbed her the next day. He didn't kill her, though. Then jumped on a plane and flew to England. He'd had it all planned out. He was eventually caught in India, where he had disguised himself by growing a beard and wearing a turban.

I know it's weird to have been around this many people who have committed such heinous acts. It's definitely not normal, unless you grew up in the projects or a ghetto in the States. I knew all of these guys, and I knew them as good people. I'm not condoning or justifying what they did, but I can't help but remember the good parts of them. That's the way I am. I can't help but see the good in people, even when I know that they're not *all* good. Every now and then I'll run into someone who knows someone who went to visit one of these guys in jail and they'll say, "Hey Russell, so-and-so said you're really popular in the joint."

The fact that this shit was all around me really freaks me out. In fact, my entire family has been shaken by all this violence because in some cases, it has hit too close to home. In 1995, I came home one night at about two or three in the morning and Dad was in his office. I said, "What are you doing up?" and he started crying and told me my cousin Andrew had been killed. Andrew had been working in the Dominican Republic. He used to host these poker games with friends in the building where he lived. One night, one of his friends parked in another guy's parking spot (somebody he'd already had a few run-ins with) and the guy went ballistic. Andrew went downstairs to talk to the guy, and as soon as he stepped out the front door, the guy pulled out a gun and shot him straight through the heart. Andrew had it all. He was good-looking, funny as hell and totally charming. He was the one person who encouraged me to become a comic. He was murdered when he was only thirty-two years old. It was the first time I had to deal with a death this close in the family, and to be honest, I don't know how I dealt with it.

After my grandparents divorced, my mother was estranged from her father for sixteen-plus years. They reconnected in the mid-'70s after her father emigrated to Australia with his second wife. Mom and my grandfather had only just reconnected. He had even sent her a care package from Australia—boomerangs, stuffed animals, Australian thermometers . . . My grandfather worked as a security guard in the Walton's department store in Sydney, and one day a young couple came in and started shoplifting. My grandfather saw them. He followed them outside and confronted the guy. The guy then proceeded to attack him. He beat my grandfather and knocked him to the ground, where he began kicking him. Nobody came to my grandfather's aid, and the couple got away. My grandfather managed to get himself back inside the department store, where he started to complain of chest pains. They called an ambulance for him, and he died of a heart attack in the ambulance on the way to the hospital as a result of the beating he'd received. The guy who beat my grandfather never went to jail for murder because there was never enough evidence to convict him.

The entire spectre of murder is a little too close to me for my own liking. It's not just knowing those who've committed these crimes, but knowing those who have been taken away so senselessly by them. The loss changes the way you see your loved ones and the world around you. I thought that after my cousin Andrew was taken away from us my association with this kind of tragedy would be over, but it wasn't the case.

After graduating from North Peel in '89, I applied to Sheridan College in Brampton. I didn't really want to go to college, because I didn't like school to begin with. But after applying, I learned that Sheridan wouldn't even accept my high school diploma because they didn't recognize my high school as acceptable. I remember thinking this was all just bullshit, that I'd agonized through math and English courses for four years only to find out that they weren't even good enough for a post-secondary education.

So what did I do? I kept really quiet about it, and when my dad gave me the money to go to school, I just headed off to college without actually being enrolled in any classes. My dad would send money off for my tuition, and when the refunds would come in the mail, I'd intercept them, take the money and spend it on other stuff.

But here's the thing: it's not like I just sat around on the couch all day. I did go to college, technically. I'd get up in the morning, then take all my records to campus with me. Sheridan had a radio station with a whole DJ setup, and I would DJ for that station all day long. That was the extent of my college education. DJ Russell on the air at the Brampton campus of Sheridan College.

"DJ Russell."

There is no shame involved in anything I did back then. I feel like I defended myself when I was picked on, made fun of, or even when I was quietly underestimated. I did what I had to do. No remorse. Actually, I remember those days fondly, because they made me who I am today. I don't feel scarred from that time in my life, probably because I've become successful since, and so, in a lot of ways, I'm able to see the past for what it was and move on.

In '97, I went back to Chinguacousy for a high school reunion. I had already done a little bit of TV, and admittedly, when I went back there, I was a really arrogant asshole. I felt like I had something to prove, and seeing the faces of those who'd treated me like garbage—who'd literally thrown me *in* the garbage—brought it all back home. But I'm glad to say that that anger didn't last.

CHAPTER 6

ONE WORD: PAKI

I HATE the word *Paki*. It's my "N" word. In case you don't know it, it's the slang term used against Indians, Pakistanis and sometimes Arabs—or anyone else from that part of the world. It started being used in England in the '70s and made its way to Canada and other parts of the Commonwealth.

The word *Paki* is one of those words that has been directed my way through all of my formative years; it's a word that followed me until I was about eighteen, and it's a word that's really hard to forget. I'm pleased to say that nowadays, Paki is not a word I hear all that often—it's faded into the background—but there are still some assholes who use it, cowards who most often will say it when they're just out of hearing range, always behind your back and rarely to your face. These days, it's a word used only when there are no Pakis around.

I associate the term with stigma and venom; it still really makes my stomach churn when I hear people using it. I don't even like it when Indian people say it. And I don't like it used, even if it's in a "nice" way. For instance, sometimes someone around me will say something like "I saw a really good Paki comic at a club last night," and I'll be fuming. Because here's the thing: if that person had seen a black comic, they would never say, "I saw a really good nigger comic last night." No way. And there's still something in that usage that is pointing to a person's feelings of superiority, as if they're subtly suggesting that it's amazing that a Paki might actually be good at something or might even be better at it than a "non-Paki." Just a few years ago, I was in a restaurant and a guy actually said to me, "Hey, you're that guy who does those Paki jokes!" I couldn't believe my ears. I just stared at him like, "Are you fucking *serious*?" So let's get this straight, once and for all: there's simply no right time or way for that word to be used.

When I was growing up and was called a Paki a lot, I learned really fast that being Pakistani has nothing to do with the power of the insult. Amazingly, your parents could be from Sri Lanka, Trinidad or, in my case, India . . . and you were still a Paki. Paki became an umbrella term for anyone who was brown, and the intent, no matter where you were

Now, I'm just five years old, I'm getting sprayed with a garden hose and I don't even have a clue what a Paki is.

from, was to make you feel like a piece of shit. There was never any good association with the word. You never heard, "Hey, that guy's a great Paki!" I don't know if Pakistani people have tried to reclaim the word for themselves, but for me, to this day, every time I hear it, I feel someone's picking at a scab.

So here's where I let you in on why. To do this, I need to take you back to the Gates of Bramalea, the complex of townhouses where I grew up. It was the summer of '75, and wee Russell Peters, five years old, was riding his bicycle through the neighbourhood. Just a kid on a bike on a nice summer day, and I rode past this house on the corner, very close to where I lived. Out on the front lawn was one of the neighbours, Mr. Gould, and he was watering his lawn with a garden hose. As I rode past, the man said to me—a five-year-old child on a bike—"Go home, you fuckin' Paki." And before I knew what was going on, he'd pointed the hose at me.

Now, I'm just five years old, I'm getting sprayed with a garden hose and I don't even have a clue what a Paki is. I was completely innocent. So in my child's mind, I looked for a way to comprehend what was going on, and so I thought to myself, *Mr. Gould, our nice neighbour, is doing me a favour. He's pointing a hose of cold water at me because it's hot outside and he's helping me cool off.*

A lot of racial abuse was directed at me as a kid, but it took a long time for me to comprehend what it all meant in the big picture. Meanwhile, my mom didn't really experience firsthand what I was going through—and that was weird, too. I mean, my mom's a hell of a lot more Indian than I am—she was born and raised in India but happens to have fair skin—and then there's me, born in Canada, and I'm the one being picked on for being from somewhere else.

On any given day, my mom would go to the bakery on Dupont Street or wherever else she needed to go; sometimes the staff in the stores would speak to her in Italian or Maltese, other times in Portuguese. They had no idea who they were talking to, so more often than not, they just kind of assumed she was one of them. I never had that feeling when I was on the streets; if I went into an Italian shop, it was clear to everyone that I was not Italian. When I went to Mom as a kid to tell her I'd been called a Paki, her response was, "Well, you just turn around and tell them that you're from India, and you're not a Paki. So there." For her, the problem was easily solved by offering a simple geography lesson, but even then, I knew there was more going on beneath the surface.

Here's a strange fact: as a kid, there were times when I never really felt close to my mom. It's hard for me to even say that because I adore her and now I'm totally a mama's boy. I actually feel I share a lot more traits with Mom than with anyone else in the family. Still, when I was young, I almost harboured resentment against her because she used to yell at me when I was a pain in the ass. I'd gotten used to being yelled at outside the home for my skin colour, so as a kid I just kind of assumed my mom was yelling at me for the same reason—for not being white. So I kind of had this little psychological problem. I don't think I really got close to my mom until I was a teenager and was old enough to realize she had had good reasons to discipline me when I was young, reasons that had nothing to do with skin tone.

In my teenage years, things kind of built up inside me, and because I didn't have much of an outlet for my rage, I eventually turned to revenge as a way of dealing with some of the bad shit that had been directed at me. Gould, my racist neighbour, was always there in the background. After he turned that hose on me when I was five and called me a "fuckin' Paki."

One night, I was walking back home through the Gates of Bramalea townhouses with Willie. I don't know why, but for some reason the entire episode of Mr. Anglo-Saxon Gould calling me a fuckin' Paki kept flashing through my mind. I'd come to know the Gould family over the years. They had two kids: a girl my brother's age, and a boy who was just one year older than me.

So Willie and I were walking by the Gould house, and as I looked up, I saw Gould in his big bay window overlooking the backyard, sitting in his living room, watching TV. I was fifteen and full of angst, and I could still remember so vividly his being such a son of a bitch, so before I could think too much about it, and before Willie could stop me, I picked up a big rock and threw it at his window. *Bam!* This meteor smashed right through as Gould was watching TV, and he stood up, and I don't think he saw us because as he went to the window, we bolted. By the time he was outside, we were nowhere to be found.

I picked up a big rock and threw it at his window. *Bam!*

The next night, I convinced Willie to return with me to the scene of the crime. I just had to get a good look at that satisfying hole in Gould's perfect little world. But the bay window had been fixed. Gould had replaced the broken glass.

A lot has changed since the late '70s. When we first moved to Brampton, it was still just a bedroom community of Scottish, Irish, English, German and Dutch immigrants. They were scared, which is ultimately what racism and prejudice is all about: fear. They were afraid of the changes that were about to come their way. They only saw the differences between "us" and "them" rather than the similarities. But as is often the case, the more time you spend with people from different backgrounds, the more you find out how similar you are.

I like to think that my act focuses on the sameness of our differences. I've been told by different fans that even though they were Greek or Italian or Lebanese, they too had a father just like mine—they too had an "Indian" father.

I know that Canadians have come a long way since back then. I see how hard they try to accept new immigrants and cultures when thirty years ago, there's no way they would have accepted them into their communities.

There's always going to be racism. We'll never get rid of it. It allows one group of people to feel superior to and more powerful than another group of people. I still see it regularly. I'm even guilty of it. I know the one thing that disappoints me these days is when I go back to Brampton and see how segregated it is. I see groups of kids hanging out only along racial lines—Indian kids with Indian kids, Filipinos with Filipinos. I understand this—the group gives everyone a sense of security and sameness—but I feel like those kids are missing out on all the other good stuff that comes from mixing with others. I feel bad for them because once they go out into the world and leave their little bubbles of sameness, they're going to be playing catch-up and will probably have some issues fitting in and getting along. They'll be no different from those white kids who didn't understand me when I first moved to Brampton. They're going to be afraid and will see only the differences instead of the similarities between all of us.

CHAPTER 7

A NINETEEN-YEAR-OLD SMART-ASS

IN 1989, I was a nineteen-year-old smart ass. I liked to joke around a lot, especially when I was with my friends and cousins. One day at my cousin Patty's apartment, I was making her son Andrew laugh. Andrew was a year older than my brother, and they were very close. Andrew was good-looking and charismatic and had a good sense of humour. He said to me, "You're pretty funny. You should go to Yuk Yuk's and try doing your jokes on stage."

Andrew's older brother Bruce chimed in, "Yeah. I can see you doing it."

I was like, "Okay." The thought had never crossed my mind, but once Andrew said it out loud, it sounded like a pretty good idea. In retrospect, it reminds me of that scene in *Friends*, when in a flashback sequence, Chandler tells Monica she should be a chef after she makes him some "righteous mac 'n' cheese." She blurts out, "Okay!"

I mentioned to my brother that this was something I was thinking of doing. At that time, I was just spinning my wheels. I wasn't in school. I was working part time, DJing. This was the closest thing I could find to a direction in life. My brother said, "Okay. I'll take you around to a couple of places and you can check it out." In September, he took me to watch an amateur night at Yuk Yuk's, just to see what it was like. A few weeks later, he went to an improv/sketch comedy show called TheatreSports on Queens Quay near Toronto's waterfront. I looked at what everyone was doing and said to myself, "I could do this."

On Tuesday, November 28, 1989, I stepped on stage for the first time. It was at the Yuk Yuk's comedy club at Yonge and Eglinton, which unfortunately closed down a few years ago. It was an amateur night with maybe fifty people in the audience. Amateur nights are free, and the audience definitely gets its money's worth . . . and not a penny more. Judy Croon MC'd, and Craig McLachlan and Jerry Moore followed with really, really bad impressions. I had a few friends with me. I had zero material. I went up there with nothing—no bits, no set, not even any premises

I went up there with nothing—no bits, no set, not even any premises to build jokes around.

to build jokes around. The club gave me five minutes, and I did two or three. I was just nervous, giggly and shitty. I have no idea what I said or did, but I got a couple of chuckles, and that was enough to get me hooked. I took my couple of chuckles and started to really think about what I needed to do the next time I went on stage. I returned to the club in February or March of 1990. This time, I'd written down some ideas and actually got some pretty good laughs. They gave me five minutes and I did maybe four.

It would be another four years before I got bumped up from amateur nights to being a feature or opener within the Yuk Yuk's group of clubs. Within the Yuk Yuk's clubs, the progression was:

1. Amateur Nights (anyone can take the stage)
2. Split Middle (two guys do ten minutes each)
3. Middle (one guy does twenty minutes)
4. Co-feature (two guys do about thirty minutes each)
5. Feature (also called a headliner in Canada: one guy does an hour)
6. "A" Feature (you're good)
7. "AA" Feature (you're really good)
8. "AAA" Feature (you're really, really good)

The pay scale back in the early '90s was: Middle, $65; MC, $75; "A" Feature, $100; "AA" Feature, $150; and "AAA" Feature, $200.

During that time, I was picking up gigs anywhere I could. Comedian Howard Dover used to run this gig in Whitby, Ontario, every Tuesday night. The gig was at this mini-putt place, and you'd perform inside this giant golf ball. We'd do the gig for free. In lieu of payment, they'd give us whatever finger foods we wanted off the menu, and then, after the show, they'd open up their go-kart track for us. So a bunch of comics would be driving go-karts around in the middle of the night. This was 1990 and I didn't have a car, so Marlon used to drive me out to that gig in his 1976 BMW 530i. Every Tuesday, he'd drive me the eighty or so kilometres to Whitby so that we could eat free finger foods and drive

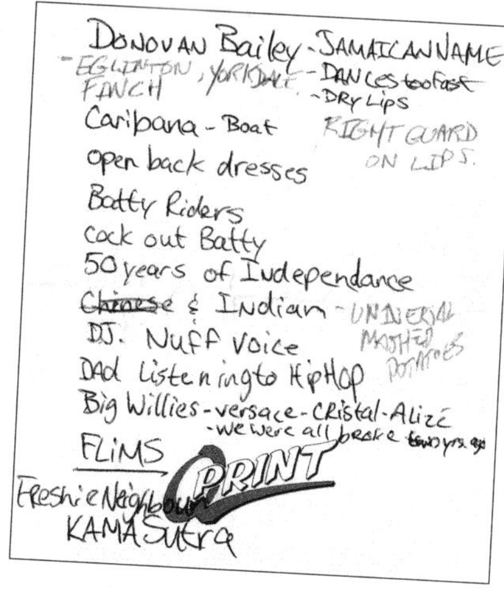

One of my early set lists.

go-karts. Howard now lives in L.A., and in 2005, when we first got down there, my brother and I hired him to drive us around to our various meetings. He knew his way around and it was pretty helpful for us to be able to get from meeting to meeting without worrying about getting lost.

That same year, 1990, I went by Yuk Yuk's in Mississauga. My material was still pretty lame at this point, but I had put together a little binder with all of my jokes. I'd written them out, word for word, on lined paper. It wasn't much, but I was pretty proud of that binder. I took that thing with me to every club. It had a Yuk Yuk's sticker right on the front. Vito, the manager of the club, was a great guy, and he agreed to give me stage time now and again, just for practice. One Saturday night, I was sitting in the greenroom with my notebook right beside me. I was young and less than a year deep in the business. I was all eager and excited. I had no idea yet that comics can be complete assholes.

So the headline comic, Boyd Coons (at that time he used his real name, which he later changed to Boyd Banks), was sitting back there with me. He was headlining that night. He had achieved a certain notoriety for his so-called edgy comedy material and had had a certain amount of success with some of his TV roles. Banks pointed to my notebook and asked, "So hey, what's that?" And I responded with, "Oh, that's my jokes." As I said before, I was pretty earnest and somewhat innocent. Then he asked if he could see them. I said, "Oh, sure man," thinking, *This is great. Here we are, two guys in the same business, helping each other out.*

He opened up my binder and started reading my jokes. He was quiet for a minute, and then he said, "You're not fucking going on our show tonight. Not with this shit." I was totally floored. I mean, here was a comic I recognized, someone I thought would show a little decency toward newcomers on the scene, and he completely trashed my set without even having seen me perform it. Banks used his pull to take me off the bill that night. I bet you that today, he doesn't even remember that he refused to let me open for him, but I sure haven't forgotten.

I picked up other gigs outside of Yuk Yuk's in small towns all over Ontario—Oshawa, Ajax, Pickering. There was a gig in the basement of a seafood restaurant in Hamilton called The Aquarium. These shows were organized by a woman named Diane, who was married to comedian Chris Pongrac. Diane made you "audition" to see if they were going to work with you. They'd make you fill out an application form, and one of the questions was "Who are your favourite comics?" After the audition and completing the application, Diane would critique your set like some kind of comedy guru. It was ridiculous. Best of all, this was a no-pay gig: your payment was dinner at the restaurant. I do remember that the restaurant had this one dish that I loved, coquille St-Jacques—it was fantastic!

I also did this Northern Ontario circuit with comedian Rob Trick, who has since become a teacher with Humber College's comedy program in Toronto, and Rob Evans, who did magic. Evans was also a high school teacher in Oshawa or Ajax. Trick had this Toyota and would drive all of us. I always appreciated Trick hooking me up with these shows, and it was pretty good money at the time. We'd start off with a gig in New Liskeard and spend the night there. The next day there'd be a show at a bar in Little Current, which should have been called "nothing current," then a gig in Sault Ste. Marie the next night and finally an eight-hour drive from there to Timmins for the final show. The gig in Timmins was in a club called the Hollywood Backlot Studios, which was a comedy club built underneath a video store. The video store and the club were owned by Syd Brooks—maybe the only Jewish guy in Timmins. Syd and his family were very nice to me and even sent me a letter telling me how great it had been to have me at their club and telling me how well I was going to do in the future.

August 23, 1993.

Dear Russell:

We thoroughly enjoyed your performance as Master of Ceremonies at our latest comedy show hosting Rob Evans and Rob Trick. The audience loved you.

You have a very promising career as a comedian and we at the Hollywood Studio Comedy Show wish you the best of luck and we look forward to your return to Timmins.

Yours sincerely,

Sydney Brooks.

SB:kdf

CHAPTER 8

I DIG CHICKS

*UNFORTUNATELY, THESE LADIES ARE JUST FANS.

WHEN I STARTED thinking about writing this book, the subject of sex was one of the first things I thought about. How was I going to talk about it? And how much detail was I going to go into? It's important to me that I'm honest with my fans, but I also realize that there are a lot of people who will get turned off by too much information on this topic.

Hopefully, the next few pages of anecdotes about my life as a normal, healthy, heterosexual male won't be too upsetting for any of the older folks reading this book. I've also tried to be a little more PG with the language than I normally would be. If you're afraid of sex or talking about sex, then skip this chapter.

I must have been maybe seven years old when I first fell in love. Her name was Connie Furtado. She was Portuguese and the same age as me. We met at a wedding—I don't remember whose wedding it was, probably someone that worked with my dad. (There were a lot of Portuguese people working at the chicken-processing plant.)

I was totally in love with Connie, but I can honestly say I don't know why. It wasn't so much that there was something about her—her smile, her sense of humour, her knowledge of KISS . . . Frankly, I have no idea what her smile was like or what she found funny or if she even liked KISS. What did I know? I was seven, for God's sake. I just remember dancing with her at the wedding and I liked the idea of being with a girl. At that time of my life, I was more in love with the idea of being in love—I was a romantic seven-year-old.

The whole concept of being a romantic at that age can be traced back to 1978 and the movie *Grease*. I was a fan of John Travolta because of the show *Welcome Back, Kotter*. I wanted to see *Saturday Night Fever*, but I was too young . . . but I could see *Grease*. *Grease* was a big romantic comedy, and I loved it. I really got into the love story between Danny Zuko and Sandy Olsen, and I ended up memorizing all of the

I must have been maybe seven years old when I first fell in love.

dialogue, the dances and the music. *Danny and Sandy—that's love,* I thought to myself. It looked really neat to me and I couldn't wait to be in love myself.

By the time I reached high school, I had been "in love" many times and seemingly had my heart broken just as often. I would let go of my romantic side after finding myself dumped repeatedly. By the time I was eighteen years old, I was five feet, ten inches tall but only about a hundred and fifty pounds. I was a late bloomer, not only genetically, but sexually. I didn't necessarily have the sex drive of an eighteen-year-old. I mean, I was sexual, but it was really all about "pleasuring myself" and not someone else. The concept of introducing *someone else* to this process never entered my mind, until . . .

I was seeing this girl—she was half-black and really pretty, with green eyes. I was living on Epsom Downs Drive (the house where my brother and I basically had the entire basement to ourselves). It was a Friday night, the day after my eighteenth birthday, and this girl and I were in my bedroom. From what she said, she was very sexual and had had a very active sex life with her ex-boyfriend, who was also an Indian guy. She really wanted to have sex with me that night, and I figured that I had to lose it at some point, so we went for it.

I was horrible and didn't even "finish." All I kept thinking was, *Man, I can't wait for her to leave so I can "manually relieve myself."* I *so* wasn't ready for sex with an actual woman. It would be twelve years before I hit my sexual stride.

My second time was with this Anglo-Indian girl. She just climbed on top and rode me for an hour. She thought that I was really good at it because I didn't "finish" as soon as we started. Fact is, I didn't finish at all. I remember that as soon as she was done, I literally rolled over and called my buddy to find out what he and I were going to do that night. I think she started crying when I got on the phone to make plans. Wow, what an asshole I was.

I fell in love, real love, for the first time in the summer of 1989. Her name was Sherrie. Actually, it wasn't, but we'll call her that. (All the women I'm naming here are aliases, by the way.) I met her at the Anglo-Indian reunion in London, and she was a total babe. I mean, really, she was Anglo-Indian and pretty—she was my ideal girl. I was completely smitten. I was eighteen and was convinced that she was the love of my life. This was it. We were going to last forever. At that age, that's how you see the world—everything is immediate, dramatic and intense.

Dancing my heart out, doing the Roger Rabbit at the Anglo-Indian reunion.

After I got back to Canada, we continued our relationship for a year, talking on the phone and writing letters to each other on an almost daily basis. This was before email, Facebook or Twitter. The whole concept of being so far apart and being able to communicate only via handwritten letters, cards and phone calls added to our "love." The excitement of getting mail from her was indescribable.

It was in the autumn of that same year that I started doing stand-up. I remember being so excited after my first open-mike night and calling her to tell her about it. She didn't really get it, but she was happy for me.

One year to the day after we first met, I decided to fly to London and surprise her for our anniversary. I borrowed four hundred dollars from my friend Paul Perliss for the ticket and told Sherrie that I was sending her a surprise for our anniversary. When she asked me what it was, I told her, "Don't worry. It's a big brown package—you'll know when it gets there." I even called her when I landed in England to ask her if it had arrived yet.

I showed up at her house and knocked on the door. She was shocked to see me, and since we were strictly communicating by letters and phone, this face-to-face meeting was a little awkward. We

Sherrie became a Muslim and ended up marrying the guy who replaced me.

sat around her parents' family room, talking and looking at photographs. At some point, she put on a video of her at some party. There were her parents, her cousins—*oh, look . . . there she is, dancing . . . Oh, now she's dancing with some guy . . . Oh, look, there she is kissing that same guy. What the fuck?* All of a sudden my world came crashing down. She admitted that she'd been seeing the guy in the video for a while and that they were serious. Everything in my world turned to shit. So much for forever. But seriously, what did I expect at eighteen? Sherrie became a Muslim and ended up marrying the guy who replaced me.

After that, I had no game and no confidence. It would be another year and a half before I even thought of kissing another girl. Aside from amateur nights, I was starting to DJ more, mostly at Indian parties. There were these "day dances" at the colleges and clubs, because the Indian girls weren't allowed to go out at night—and that's where I met "Brenda." Brenda was almost the same age as me, and we started seeing each other for about a year and a half. She was Hindu and her parents were crazy-strict. For the entire duration of our relationship, they never even knew I existed or that she had a boyfriend.

Brenda would stay overnight at my place, despite her parents. She'd tell them that she was staying at her cousin's place. If her parents called her cousin, her cousin would call my house, and then she'd call her parents back. It was the first time that I was getting laid on a regular basis, and I'd like to think that I was finally getting better at it. At the same time, Brenda and I were both twenty-one and were filled with that kind of crazy twenty-one-year-old psychotic relationship stuff—full of paranoia, jealousy and insecurity.

We stayed together for about eighteen months, until I met Jeanette. Like Sherrie, Jeanette was another Anglo-Indian beauty, and I was completely enamoured with her from the moment we met. We were together only for a few weeks, but it was the first time that I'd forgotten about Sherrie in two years. However, like my relationship with Sherrie, this one was doomed.

One night, I was trying to get in touch with her but couldn't find her. I ended up driving past her house and saw her ex-boyfriend's car in the driveway. I was pissed, so I drove around some more before I returned to her place. The car was gone and I went in to see her. The first thing out of my mouth was "I saw Roger's car." She didn't deny it. Then I asked the gayest thing ever: "Did you *kiss*?"

"Yes," she replied, and I walked out quietly.

I was so pissed off that I actually hated her. And when I say I "hated her," I mean I really *hated* her. The hate was completely disproportionate, of course, but it was totally in keeping with how I reacted to everything in my early twenties. Eventually, I stopped hating her and we became friends.

Jeanette had a cousin named Angela who she said really liked me, so I started seeing her. She was a nice girl from a nice family. The only problem was that I was no longer a nice guy. I'd been hurt twice and wasn't ready to fully commit. Looking back, I was completely immature, too. Within the first year of us being together, I had started to fool around on her. I was doing stand-up and DJing a lot and was starting to become a "name." My DJ name was the very imaginative DJ Russell and I was playing a lot of Indian parties, where I had a lot of chicks throwing themselves at me—which was completely new to me. I was never hot with the ladies before, and so I took full advantage of it. I'd also never hung around Indian people before, and it was all new to me. Angela had no desire to come to any of the parties and preferred to stay home. I, on the other hand, was going out all the time.

I was a punk. I was screwing around with girls all over the place.

I had no sense of consequences and no consideration for other people's feelings. I was a punk. I was screwing around with girls all over the place, getting into fights and completely selfish. Over the six years we were together, I screwed around A LOT. Angela suspected that I was screwing around, and so did her friends and family. Thing was, I told myself that I could do anything I wanted and that she was never going to leave me. By the end of our relationship, her family hated me.

In 1996, I met this girl named Rachel at a Christmas party. She was this ridiculously hot, half-black/half-Chinese chick and—oh my God—I had never met a girl this pretty before. Even more incredible was that she was actually into *me*. I was still with Angela and broke up with her to go out with Rachel. Two weeks after we broke up, I called Angela and she was crying. It's not like there was call display. I just called and she was crying. I was like, *Wow! She really loves me!* So we got back together. But the thing is, I never broke up with Rachel. Rachel and I were still together and would remain together for the next two years. Over those two years, I was seeing both Angela and Rachel. Angela's parents lived in the west end of the city and had a rule that I had to leave their house by ten-thirty at night. Rachel was a nurse and lived in the east end of the city. After leaving Angela's, I'd drive east and pick up Rachel after she finished her shift. I'd spend the rest of the night with her and end up back in Brampton by four in the morning.

My parents never liked Rachel. She thought it was because she was half-black, but she was wrong. It was actually because she was "the other woman." I mean, Dad did call her The Blink—because of her being black and Chinese. When she'd call, my dad would yell out, "Russell, The Blink is on the phone!" Whenever I'd go out to clubs and parties, I'd always bring Rachel with me. Nobody even knew about Angela—she never wanted to go out anyway. Even if she did want to go out, I was such an asshole that I literally made her stay home.

Eventually, it all came crashing down around me. One day, while we were broken up over something stupid, Angela came over to my parents' house. While I was in the shower, she was waiting for me in my room. As she waited, she came across this shoebox filled with tons of pictures of me and Rachel, plus pics of me and other chicks from

Ireland, England and other parts of the world. There were also letters and cards from various women—my entire cheating hard drive.

I came out of the bathroom and she told me that she had to leave. I didn't think anything of it, until she just stopped coming around and stopped phoning. Christmas came and she wasn't there, then New Year's. It was weird, and I panicked. It was more ego than anything—I was no longer in control. I was depressed and even ended up breaking up with Rachel because I wanted to get back together with Angela, but it was too late. She'd already moved on and started seeing another guy, whom she ultimately married . . . What am I? Russell Peters, last stop before marriage?

In December 2001, I met Shivani, whom I call "Beauts." I was hosting a show at the Hummingbird Centre in Toronto, where she was presenting something. She wore a sash that said MISS INDIA-CANADA BEAUTY PRINCESS. It was the funniest title I'd ever seen, but I thought she was cute and wanted to meet her. By May 2004, I got engaged to Shivani. At the time, it seemed like the right thing to do. I really, really loved her and still love her to death. But we got engaged for all the wrong reasons. My dad had died two months earlier, and I thought that getting engaged would cheer up my mom. Plus, I saw marrying Shivani as a tribute to my dad, who also loved her a lot. Dad's hearing was pretty bad, and when my brother or I would refer to her as "Beauts," he thought we were saying "Buick." He ended up calling her Buick until the day he died.

She is a sweet girl and gorgeous, too—perfect in every way—but for someone else. Unfortunately for me, our relationship had shifted from lovers to friends. I'd developed a whole Madonna-Whore complex and just couldn't shake it. We broke up in September of 2004 because I knew that it wasn't going to work out in the long run.

I never once fooled around on Shivani. But we did break up a few times during our relationship, and then I'd fuck around like crazy until we got back together. That I still love Shivani to death has been a sore point for some of the girls I've gone out with since.

The breakup with Shivani coincided with the great leap forward in my career. I was sleeping with a lot of women at that point but was putting most of my energy into my stand-up. I wasn't interested in having a girlfriend or a long-term relationship. I was on the road non-stop and was having a great time in every city I went to. I had my first threesome in San Francisco—it was great.

I even dated a porn star, Sunny Leone, who was actually a really cool chick. She was smoking hot. We met in Sacramento the night before I taped *Outsourced*. We started dating about two years later. Now, when I say she was a porn star, I should mention that her thing was strictly girl-on-girl stuff. There were no guys involved. While we were going out, she went on *The Howard Stern Show* and told them that she was seeing a guy who had given her the best sex she'd ever had (ahem, me!!!!). Sunny was a great girl and we had a good time together. We broke up when she decided to start doing guy-girl sex in her movies. I mean, here's the thing: when most women come home from work, their feet are sore . . .

In those early L.A. years I just wanted to learn the lay of the land (excuse the pun). I'm a normal heterosexual man, so I did what I needed to do. I dated a few different girls, but it didn't take long for me to find myself with an actual "girlfriend." "Kelly" worked at the Beverly Center, which is where I met her while buying shoes for Shivani. (Shivani and I had not been together for years at that point, but I must admit that I continued to buy her gifts whenever I got the chance just because she'd been there when I was broke.)

Kelly was Cuban and Salvadorian and was really pretty. She wasn't the brightest girl (Paris Hilton was her idol), and the stuff that she used to say made me laugh—which isn't an easy thing to do. Sometimes I'd meet girls who thought they were funny and would try to be funny with me, and it never worked. Kelly was incidentally funny. Even though Kelly was born and raised in the States, she completely mangled the English language. She was a master of malapropisms without even knowing it. She once referred to Martin Luther

King Day as *Martha* Luther King Day, and instead of Copenhagen, she referred to it as Coco Heaven. She usually knew she was screwing things up and never tried to hide it, which I always liked about her. My family was a bit suspicious of Kelly since she was my first real girlfriend since Shivani. They thought she was with me only for my money and didn't trust her. My mom wasn't very nice to her when they met. Mom wouldn't even look at her when we had dinner together—but then again, my mom's pretty leery of any women I bring around. My brother, who has no threshold for people who can't speak properly or whom he doesn't find very bright, wasn't that nice to her either.

We had a rollercoaster relationship, and when we broke up, she didn't take it well. One night I came home and was getting ready for bed. It must have been around four in the morning. I opened the closet door and she leapt out! She scared the shit out of me and I flipped out. She had broken into the house via my bathroom window, which was about twenty-five feet from the ground but parallel to the neighbour's driveway support wall, which was about three feet away. She jumped from the wall to the bathroom window—which I had left open. She crawled in. If she'd fallen, she could have broken her neck.

Two Christmases ago, she jumped on a plane and came to see me in Toronto. She wasn't going to leave until we got back together. I guess when you're in your early twenties, this seems like a good idea—romantic and spontaneous. It actually sounds like something I would have done at that age. I get it. But when you actually *do* it, it's completely impractical. She had no return ticket and two suitcases full of her stuff. I guess if we had gotten back together it would have been a great story to tell on *Oprah*—"That's right, Oprah. I just showed up at his house and told him that I loved him and wasn't going to leave until he took me back!"

"You go, girl!" Oprah would have answered.

Unfortunately, that wasn't the case. I was cold and distant and had her back on a plane to L.A. within seventy-two hours.

Here's the thing: I don't think Mom is going to like *any* girl I bring home.

We were on and off for a while after that, but it all ended when I met Amanda. Amanda was twenty-two years old and worked at a shoe store at Yorkdale Mall in Toronto. To me, Amanda looked like Phoebe Cates in *Fast Times at Ridgemont High* (which was made six years before she was even born). She was half-Italian and half-Chilean and had no interest in me, which only made me want her more. I ended up calling her and we went out. She was really pretty, and I was really into her, far more than she was into me. Even though our age difference was the same as the age difference between my parents, my mom thought she was too young for me and was, once again, not very welcoming to her. "I was a much more mature twenty-two-year-old," she'd say to me.

Here's the thing: I don't think Mom is going to like *any* girl I bring home. She doesn't care about any girl I claim to be serious about unless that girl works in a K-mart cafeteria and has a high-school education. Being short, plain-looking and simple would probably help, too. Like I've said before, I'm a mama's boy and let my mom get away with a lot. She's definitely enjoying a very comfortable lifestyle now and doesn't have to worry about anything—which I love, because, well, she's my mom. But she reminded both Kelly and Amanda, "You may be his girlfriend but I'm always going to be his mother." Mom may give off a folksy demeanour, but don't be fooled—she knows exactly what she's doing. It's going to take a very special woman to know how to handle her and still remain in her good books.

Amanda and I had a very intense relationship as well. But it was filled with the same stuff that I went through in my early twenties—paranoia, insecurity, jealousy and those stupid fights that you mistake for passion at that age. "I've just never loved somebody this much before and it scares me"—that type of thing. I was trying to convince myself that she was the one. I'm not an argumentative guy, especially with a woman because—let's be honest, guys—you can't win an argument with a woman. Unfortunately, at the time, she couldn't control her own temper and the fights became more and more public, at which point I had to get away from the situation. It was poison.

I mean, ultimately, at the end of the day, I'm not different from any other human being on the planet. I just wanted to be loved and I wanted to love someone. Throughout all of these women, all I was ever looking for was love. And yeah, sure I slept around and had threesomes and did whatever I had to or was able to do or was afforded to me from the profession I had chosen. If I was still Russell, the guy that worked in the mall, none of these opportunities would have presented themselves, and I wouldn't be writing this book because it would be a pretty boring story. But at the end of the day, all I ever wanted to do was find that one and now I think I'm lucky to have found her. Also, that's why it's easier for me to write this paragraph now because I know that this is all behind me and that it's a different life ahead of me for the next forty years.

In July of 2010, I got engaged to a beautiful Latina from Los Angeles, Monica Diaz. I must admit that I've known Monica for only six months, but it didn't take long to realize that she's the one. . . . I'll tell you more in the back of this book.

PART THREE GET UP,

STAND UP

I SAW A WHITE GUY DRIVING A CAB THE OTHER DAY. WHO THE HELL DO THESE WHITE PEOPLE THINK THEY ARE COMING OVER HERE AND STEALING OUR JOBS?

CHAPTER 9

GEORGE CARLIN

I MET GEORGE CARLIN on October 24, 1992. It was a day after my dad's birthday—which, to be honest, wasn't a big deal to me at the time, not the way it is now. That night, in Atlanta, the Toronto Blue Jays won the World Series against the Braves, and as is the case when Toronto celebrates anything—the Grey Cup, hockey playoffs (minus the Stanley Cup because, well, we haven't won one since 1967), the fans poured onto Yonge Street. I was one in a crowd of thousands of people who were out there partying and going wild in celebration of the big win.

I was with all my friends, walking on Yonge Street just north of College when this old guy walked past me, and he looked just like George Carlin. Being a smart-ass, I yelled out, "Hey, how ya doin', George?" And then I realized it wasn't just that this guy *looked* like George Carlin, he *was* George Carlin. Holy shit! I was completely freaked out. My eyes were probably popping halfway out of my head.

I realized it wasn't just that this guy *looked* like George Carlin, he *was* George Carlin.

I immediately ditched all my friends and worked my way against the throng of humanity, trying to catch up with Carlin. Next thing I knew, there he was right beside me. I heard myself asking him, "What are you doing here?"

And he said, "What, am I not supposed to be here?"

And I started babbling on, saying, "Oh my god, oh my god. Wait!" And then I went on about how I've got a mix tape in my car with dubs from one of his records and how I really wanted him to hear it. And this was all true, by the way: I had taken bits of his comedy material—a line from one bit and another from something else—and laid it over a hip-hop beat. So at this point, I was so excited and nervous that I didn't know whether to shit or wind my watch. But somehow, I managed to say to George—to George *Carlin!!*—"So, can I walk you to your hotel?" And he said sure.

So Carlin and I walked together to his hotel, and I'm sure I barely stopped talking the whole way. When we got there, we hung out for a bit and he gave me an autograph. I still have that autograph, and it means the world to me that this man—one of the top names in comedy—took the time to be generous to some no-name kid he ran into on the street.

George was the nicest guy in the world to me that night, and he gave me the best advice that I ever got about comedy. He told me to get on stage as much as I could, wherever I could. He said, "It doesn't matter when, how, where, just get up there and try it." He told me that if you're at a bar and there's a band playing and they take a break, you should ask them if you can have a couple minutes on stage while they're resting. He put into my head that night, at such a young age, that comedy was a craft, that is was something you could actually get better at with practice.

After receiving his advice, all I could think to offer in return was, "My mom makes really good Indian food. I can drive you back to our place and she'll cook you up a great meal." I was such a geek and really had no clue about anything at the time, but George was just pure goodness. He turned down the dinner invite graciously. Before I left, I said to him, "Hey, maybe one day we'll work together," and he said to me, as though it were as probable as the next sunrise, "Maybe, kid. You never know."

In July of 2007, comedy legend George Carlin was not well. He had just gotten out of the hospital from having surgery and was doing some tune-up shows before he taped an HBO special. One of these shows was happening in L.A. at the Hermosa Beach Comedy and Magic Club, and knowing that I've always been a huge fan of Carlin's, the manager of the club asked me if I wanted to be part of his show. My answer? "Can I please, *please* host the show?"

The long and the short of it: they let me host for George Carlin. And that night, when I got on stage to introduce him, I couldn't help it—I got all teary-eyed. I told the audience the story about when I was a kid and met him on the streets and what a great guy he had been, how totally nice he had been to me for no good reason. Then,

George came out and, laughing, he said, "You're embarrassing me, kid. I'm not that nice."

That night was one I'll never forget. I had come full circle and gotten to share the stage with my hero. I was so happy to be there with him. I took a picture with George after the show, and I'm sure glad I did.

George passed away ten months later, in June 2008. The world lost not only one of the best comics to ever grace a stage, but a man with uncommon human decency and a really big heart.

From that first encounter with George when I was a young aspiring comic, I took his advice. I picked up every gig that I could—anytime, any place. There were gigs at reggae parties, where they'd just stop the music and put me on in the middle of the dance floor. These kinds of gigs continued well into the mid-'90s. Different promoters ran different events at clubs around Toronto. One of them, Carlos, used to run Studio 69 at Bathurst and King streets on Saturday nights. He'd pay me a hundred and fifty bucks and it would be the same thing: the music would stop, I'd stand in the middle of the dance floor and do fifteen minutes. It was a lot of fun.

By 1992 I had managed to pick up enough gigs to save three thousand dollars. I was still living at home and would continue to do so for another nine years. Dad made me pay rent of maybe two hundred dollars a month, since I was now "working." I decided that I wanted to buy my own car and set my sights on a new Saturn SL, the base model—as base as you can get with a car. It had no cassette deck, no power windows, no air conditioning, a manual transmission, and it had only one mirror on the driver's side. That car cost nine thousand dollars. I paid three and my dad kicked in the other six, which he made me pay back at two hundred dollars a month. He also kicked in a little extra so that I could get the other side mirror. Now the car looked like an SL1 instead of an SL, because it had two mirrors. I loved that car and drove the shit out of it. When I got rid of it in 1995, it had 240,000 kilometres on it—all of them gig miles.

By 1993, I was starting to feel a little cocky about my talents as a comic. I'd just come off a string of good shows. A good friend of mine, Jonathan Ramos, had set up his own promotion company, REMG Entertainment, and asked me if I'd like to open for the hip-hop group the Pharcyde, who were hot at the time with the single "Passin' Me By." The gig was at the Opera House in Toronto. I was really excited about the show because I'd grown up as a hip-hop head and I was finally getting to go on stage with rappers. I walked out on stage, and instead of hearing applause or even any sort of reaction from the crowd, all I got was silence.

When I started into my set, I was already off. My timing had been thrown by the lack of warmth in the room and it just went downhill from there. The crowd gave me some negative energy the second I took the stage. I expected them to like me automatically when I stepped out, and so I'd forgotten the important rule that as a comic, it's your job to *make* them like you, no matter what. I had about a minute in which to fight back and command their respect, but I didn't.

At the Opera House, bombing.

The next thing I knew, the crowd had gotten away from me—they were hip-hop kids and backpackers, black, white and Asian. It literally felt like I was dying on stage, that they'd have to peel me off the floorboards and put me directly into a coffin. When they started booing, it was all over, before I'd even had time to figure out what hit me.

I remember walking backstage and I wanted to cry. My mouth went dry and I thought, *This is it. My career's over.* Looking back on this moment, I've learned from my mistakes. Today, I know that the audience's reaction was fair and that I should have fought harder to earn their respect. I see lots of up-and-comers in the business who haven't learned that yet. Every fighter gets knocked down at some point—Joe Louis, Lennox Lewis. It teaches you to train more, to keep throwing punches and to always have your guard up.

Believe me, when you get booed off stage, it's not an experience you want repeated. When a boxer gets punched in the chin, that first chin check determines how it's going to be from there on. Will he lose it and get knocked out, or is he going to stand back up and fight? That show was my chin-check moment, and every comic needs one in their career to test what he or she's made of. It took me years to get over that show, but I was determined to never let it happen again, especially in front of a largely black audience. I was going to win over those audiences in the future.

By 1995, things started to change for me. After four years of steady gigging, my set had grown to thirty minutes. Of that thirty, I had polished a solid fifteen minutes. Everyone said that I had polished it so well that for fifteen minutes I could smoke anybody. In '95 I was also moved up from amateur to middle and sometimes co-headliner, depending on the gig and who else was on the show. I was now on the circuit. What's "the circuit"? you ask. Well, the circuit is any bar in any small town in Canada—O'Toole's, Bailey's Balloon Brigade, a Holiday Inn banquet hall—wherever Yuk Yuk's could undersell a gig, they would do it. They would sell a three-man comedy show for around five hundred bucks (or at least that's what the comics would see on paper). Of the five hundred bucks, I would maybe get a hundred, sometimes fifty, sometimes thirty-five. The rest would be split among the other comics. The headliners in those days were guys like Larry Horowitz, Lawrence Morgenstern, Mike Bullard and Jeremy Hotz. They would make the most—anywhere from two hundred to two hundred and fifty bucks at these road gigs.

I also recorded my first comedy special that year for CBC. They did a series of half-hour specials called *Comics*. It consisted of stand-up, sketches and B-roll (extra footage). Because of the way the show was structured, I could do my solid fifteen minutes and fill the rest of the show with sketches and other filmed bits. This was a fun special to shoot. I used my mother in some of the sketches, as well as friends of mine. In one of the filmed sketch bits, I'm standing in a bus shelter with a couple of my Indian buddies and a white guy steps in. All of a sudden, we start holding our noses and I mutter, "Jeez . . . smells like Kraft Dinner . . ." People loved that bit. The other bit consisted of me going into a store (I think we used Adventure Electronics on Yonge Street) and this guy comes up to me to help me. We used this comic Brad Lyons, who was all tall and gangly. He steps away and another white guy comes up to me. This guy's a short, stocky guy. I call him by the same name as the first guy, and he goes, "Oh, I'm not Bill, I'm Fred." And I say, "Jeez, all these people look alike to me."

I was quite proud of those sketches. That was the first time I'd gotten on TV nationally, and two things happened—CBC got a ton of fan mail for me and they got a wave of people threatening to boycott the CBC, calling me racist and unfunny. One of the very vocal critics was this guy who ran an "Indian" newspaper in Vancouver. My intentions were never to offend anybody. I got hold of the guy's phone number and called him because I wanted to know what problems he had with my act. I remember I called him from the speakerphone in my dad's home office. He was just yelling at me, because he was really offended by this joke about Indian names, specifically Sukdip, which is pronounced "Sukdeep." Part of the bit goes like this: a guy, speaking in an angry black guy's voice, says, "Yo! I'm lookin' for Sukdeep!" and the Indian guy (with a thick accent) goes, "Well, okay, but only if I have to . . . " Not exactly gold here, folks.

Anyhow, this guy actually knew somebody named Sukdip and was really offended on his behalf. He was also really lippy, threatening to go to his member of Parliament and complain and start a full-on boycott of the CBC. He was yelling at me on the phone, and my brother overheard. Brother came in and started in on him. Brother, despite his best efforts, can't manage his temper when it comes to me or anyone in our family.

He goes from being this quiet, funny guy to an absolute pit bull. The guy on the phone got more heated. A year later, I heard he was shot dead on his doorstep. I guess I wasn't the first person he mouthed off to.

Andrew Clark of *Eye Weekly*, the free Toronto weekly newspaper, in his review of the year in comedy, said that *Comics*, the little show that could, trudged on and moved forward with some real highs (Mark Farrell) and some real lows (Russell Peters). I never forgot that because I was like, *What a dick*! I don't know what Mark Farrell and Andrew Clark are doing now. I got paid $3,500 or $5,000 or something, and I would keep getting residual cheques all the time. I remember calling the CBC every time the show would air: "Is there a cheque there for me?" And then I would run and get it. It got to the point where I knew the name of the guy in accounting: Roland, who was this older black guy. I'd just call him directly and he'd take care of me.

I continued to gig locally and, because of my special, I had a bit more credibility. I was also starting to establish myself within the black community in Toronto and across Canada. I had been playing Kenny Robinson's Nubian Disciples of Pryor, an all-black comedy night at Yuk Yuk's. The show was held on the first Sunday of every month and was always sold out. Although billed as an "all-black" show, I was on it as part of the original lineup, along with Trinidadian and other non-black comics. This was a show where the audience had adopted a hard-line attitude about what they found funny, and if they didn't like you, they'd let you know. I saw dozens of guys booed off that stage. Funny guys like Mistah Mo would kill one week and then get booed off the next. I remember him leaving the stage, yelling, "You can't boo me! Last time you loved me! You can't boo me this time!" The crowd was merciless. Somehow, I managed to hold my own with them and they took me in as one of their own.

And that's where my first wave of support came from: the black Caribbean community in Canada. I've never forgotten that.

CHAPTER 10

TOP OF THE HEAP

NEW YORK CITY first called out to me when I was twenty-one years old, and I decided to get on a bus from Toronto to see what it was like for myself. I had no money, and no real plan. But in my mind, I was thinking that I'd just show up at HBO's offices and they'd give me a gig . . .

New York City was the backdrop to the hip-hop lifestyle that I would come to define myself by: the beats, the clothing, breakdancing and graffiti. It was a mythic place that captured my imagination at a very formative time in my life. New York is the home of hip-hop. It's also the home of stand-up comedy—where the early comedians of the twentieth century were actually masters of ceremonies in the vaudeville theatres, telling jokes between variety acts.

When I finally got to Manhattan after about ten or eleven hours on the bus, my luggage had disappeared. Apparently, a woman got off the bus in Buffalo with my bag and realized it only once she got home. The bus company gave me a cheque for a hundred bucks to help me get a few things that I was going to need—a toothbrush, shampoo . . . underwear. My suitcase showed up a day later, after the woman who accidentally took it found my brother's contact details on the luggage tag and called him. I couldn't afford a hotel, especially in Manhattan, and stayed for a week at my uncle's place on Long Island. Mostly I went record shopping, where I grabbed records by Brand Nubian and Chubb Rock. I could have bought them at home, but buying them in New York made them seem that much more "authentic."

I never did make it to HBO's offices, but I did do a couple of open mikes at the New York City Comedy Club and Stand-Up New York. The shows were unmemorable and there was barely anyone in the crowd. At the end of the week, I took the bus back home. I didn't feel good or bad about the trip, but I was glad I went and saw what it was like to perform there. I also got something of a feel for the city that had spawned so much of what I loved.

Five years later, I returned to New York. I'd moved up from amateur nights and had about an hour's worth of material. I remember that I'd just finished a weekend of co-headlining with comedian Rob Ross at Yuk Yuk's in Mississauga. Even though we were co-headlining, he didn't want to follow me, so I closed every night. After the Sunday night show, I got into my Isuzu Rodeo and drove to NYC. I was going to be staying with comedian Keith Robinson, who I'd met a year earlier when he was acting in the movie *Rebound: The Legend of Earl "The Goat" Manigault*, which was filmed in Toronto. That summer, we also hung out at the Just for Laughs Festival in Montreal. Keith's a great guy and was very generous with me. "Why don't you come to New York?" he asked me. "Come stay with me in Woodbridge, New Jersey. Sleep on my couch, nigga . . . if you don't mind?" I was like, "Hell yeah!"

I drove by myself, and for some reason I remember seeing a ton of dead deer on the highway on the way there. By the time I got to New Jersey, it was rush hour and I was starting to fall asleep at the wheel, but I made it to Keith's apartment and stayed on his couch for the rest of the week.

"Some guy named Dave Chappelle asked for your number."

I brought a VHS copy of my CBC *Comics* episode with me to New York. I was really proud of that show and played it for Keith and his roommates, comics Romont Harris and Rocky. They watched it and declared, "That was shit!" They weren't just breaking balls the way comics do; they meant it. They were being honest with me, with my best interests at heart. "Nigga, anybody could do those jokes. You gotta do shit that only you can do." Keith's words stuck with me. Essentially, he was telling me what no one else had up until that point: speak in your own voice, so that it's your voice only and unique to you. He didn't want me doing generic material that could come out of any comic's mouth. That's when I changed up my style.

That week, Keith got me stage time at the Comic Strip, the Comedy Cellar, the Boston Comedy Club and Stand-Up New York. At Stand-Up New York, we ran into Dave Chappelle. I'd met Dave for the first time that summer at Just for Laughs. I was already a big fan—I'd even told him so when we first met. Dave was really nice to me from the get-go, and that was cool. In 1997, he was in Toronto filming *Half Baked* and we hung out. In fact, he went to Yuk Yuk's looking for me. I got to the club late that night, and someone mentioned that "some guy named Dave Chappelle asked for your number, so we gave it to him." I was like, "What? You're sure?" I eagerly awaited Dave's call. One night I took him for a drive to Brampton. We drove on this hilly road, Forks of the Credit Road (known locally as "Rollercoaster Road"). He loved it. He joked that I was taking him to the country to kill him. As part of his Brampton experience, we stopped off for a coffee at the Tim Hortons at Highway 10 and Bovaird Drive. We hung out quite a bit that summer.

Me and Dave Chappelle, in 1996.

While we were at the Comic Strip, Chris Rock rolled up to the club in a limo. He was still on *Saturday Night Live* at the time. He'd also been in *CB4*, *Boomerang* and, of course, *New Jack City*. I knew who he was and could see who he was going to be. Funny thing was, I didn't bother to watch his set that night. I had seen his stand-up special, *Born Suspect*, and thought it was just okay, plus I'd gotten bumped because he'd shown up, so I guess I was a little pissed. I ended up hanging out at the bar at the back of the club with Keith and the guys, talking shit and making fun of each other. Since that night, however, I've become a huge fan of Chris's work and have met him a few times. He always

Chris Rock (with his old teeth) and me, in 1996.

calls me by my full name, as in "Russell Peters!" Having someone of his stature recognize you and call you out by your full name is a form of acknowledgment that lets you know he recognizes your accomplishments.

On my last Saturday in New York, I did sets at the Boston Comedy Club and Stand-Up New York. Both shows had gone really well and I was feeling pretty good about myself. I knew that there was a gig at the Bronx BBQ—literally a barbeque restaurant—that paid $75, which was a lot of money for a spot in New York at that time. I started bugging Keith to take me out to the gig. He looked at me and said, "Nigga, you're going to get kicked in your fuckin' throat at that club."

"Come on, it's the only spot paying any money tonight!" I said. Keith took me to the show. It was an all-black room and was hosted by a comic named Capone. The first guy up was Jimmy Martinez. The audience started booing him. "Y'all niggas think this shit is easy?!" he screamed at the crowd. "I'll fight anyone of you muthafuckas!"

The second guy went up, Wild Will. Capone's introduction went like this, "Hey y'all, do you wanna see Wild Will?" The audience clapped and cheered for him. Will was kind of a weird guy—kind of crazy, really. When the crowd went nuts, I was thinking, *Wow, they must really love him.* He got up there and started doing this strange thing, the booing started and Will slunk off stage. Hmmmm . . .

So I was the third guy. I got up on stage and as soon as I started, so did the booing. I was done, booed right off stage. When I stepped off, there was Keith. "Just like I said. They kicked you in your throat!!!"

In 2004, I did a tour called The Gurus of Comedy. We did a few different cities across the U.S. But I have to admit that this time was a bit of a blur to me. Dad had just died and I was still pretty dazed. I ended up doing a solo show at the New York Improv for this wig-wearing douchebag Indian promoter in New York. This fucking guy told me he was taping my show for archiving purposes . . . and I believed him. Next thing you know, he'd uploaded the whole thing on the Web to build up his name. It really burned my ass. By dumping that show on the Web, he killed a good chunk of the new material that I was still working out. I just stopped doing a lot of those bits because of that.

It's impossible for some people to understand what it's like to have material that you didn't authorize distributed without your permission. Let's say I'm having an off night or I'm still working on new material and it gets uploaded on the Web. There's a couple of things can happen:

1) People see it and say it's shit, which kills my business.

2) People see it and expect to see new material from me when they see me live shortly thereafter.

Comedy is all about the element of surprise. If you've already seen it on the Internet, where's the surprise when you see it live?

A lot of times I've had people tell me that by putting my copyrighted material on the Web, they're helping promote me. Well, um, thanks, but I'm not looking for promotion. I appreciate that my real fans are passionate about me and want to share me with their friends, but that's not the way to do it.

The Web's been good to me, and I don't deny that. I wouldn't be where I am without that exposure—absolutely not. I'd still be playing clubs in Northern Ontario. But now I spend my own money to produce my specials and my own DVDs. If my stuff gets out there for free, I'll just have to stop coming out with new product because I won't be able to afford to do it any longer. Sorry for the rant here, but I know that there's a lot of kids out there who don't get that it costs a lot of money to make my stand-up specials and that it takes at least one year to come up with a new set and at least two years before it's ready for broadcast.

Ahem, back to New York . . . After playing the Apollo in 2005, I locked in a role in the movie *Quarter Life Crisis*. I played a shady TV producer masquerading as a limo driver who's secretly filming the lead character's love life as it unfolds in the back seat of my limo. The movie starred Maulik Pancholy, who's now a regular on one of my favourite shows, *30 Rock*, and Lisa Ray, who grew up in the Toronto suburb of Etobicoke, which also happens to be where my cousins grew up. To be honest, I never even read the entire script. It was really just a great opportunity to spend time in New York and work on a movie. The movie itself was an indie film and didn't have a big budget. We shot all over Manhattan, including a scene where I'm driving a bicycle rickshaw through Times Square at night with the two leads in the back. It was actually kind of cool. I spent about a month on the movie and really got to know Manhattan.

In November 2006 I played my first big New York shows, two back-to-back sold-out gigs at the Beacon Theatre—the same theatre where Martin Scorsese shot the Rolling Stones' *Shine a Light*. *Outsourced* had just come out in September, and this was my first large solo theatre show in New York. Almost six thousand people showed up, a really good mix of people in the audience—Indian, black, Latino, white, Chinese, Asian and Arab. Having a good mix of people at my shows is very important to me. It really allows me to dig into my material and do my best to please everyone.

The shows were fantastic and I had a really good time. It was the first show where I used a DJ on stage with me. The DJ that night was one of my best friends, New York City's DJ Spinbad. His job was to spin during the walk-in (when the audience is coming into the theatre and getting seated) and to play me on after my introduction.

Spin is a very sweet guy whom I had met a couple of years earlier. He was a regular DJ on Power 105.1 in New York. Back in the '90s, I used to pick up his mixtapes in Toronto. We chatted on the phone a few times back then, and within a very short period of time we became very, very good friends. He is one of the finest turntablists in the world. I've been with him at a club, and in the middle of having a conversation and a drink, he's just scratching, cutting and mixing away without

When I ask someone to open for me, it's important that they're good and that they get the audience warmed up.

any effort whatsoever. He makes it look effortless and does things that I can only dream of doing.

Craig Robinson, who plays the warehouse foreman in *The Office*, was one of my openers that night. The audience loved him. Craig is one of the nicest guys I know—very mellow and chill. He does his act with his electric piano, and one of the great things about him opening is that he gets a lot of the "sillies" out of the audience. He forces them to focus and settle in for when I take the stage. That's not to say that Craig's not a headliner unto himself—not at all. I've had Craig on several of my shows and he's never let me down. He's become a really good actor and is now a regular in all of the Judd Apatow movies. The one thing you'll notice in all of his acting work is not just how funny he is, but also how vulnerable his characters are. He brings another layer to his performances, which isn't easy in comedy. I also had Keith Robinson open for me that night. It had been ten years since I'd spent that week sleeping on his couch, and it was great to have him there for my first big New York show.

When I ask someone to open for me, it's important that they're good and that they get the audience warmed up. I've had guys ask me if they should go a little light with the audience—in other words, not necessarily bring their A game. No way. I want guys who are better than me and who will kill when they go on stage. I want them to make the audience forget about me. I'm a competitive guy; most comics are. I want someone who's going to force me to step up my game. I want to them to make me better, and they can't do that if they're just rolling over or weak. I know some headliners will actually ask guys to go easy when they get out there, but I go the other way and encourage the opener to really go for it.

It was at the Beacon show that I first met one of my heroes, Melle (pronounced Mel-lee) Mel of Grandmaster Flash and the Furious Five. A friend of mine had met him earlier that year and invited him down to the show. I was so blown away by having him there that I can't even describe it. He was all smiles and charm and honestly seemed to be enjoying my adulation, which I just couldn't hide. He hung out with me during the autograph session after the show, and I was a bit disappointed but not surprised by how many of the younger fans had no idea who he was. I forget that not everyone has the same reverence for the history of hip-hop as I do.

Me and my hero, Melle Mel.

After the show, all my New York crew, which we call "The Vipers," went to the club Pacha NYC on West Forty-sixth Street. The name comes from an episode of *The Sopranos* in which Tony and Christopher rip off two bikers from a gang called the Vipers. The members of the Vipers are DJs, cops, radio guys and video directors. I love these guys. There's no ego, no attitude and definitely no drama, plus we're totally uncool when you get right down to it. These guys provide me with a bit of a safety zone when we're together. I can do silly things with them—I can drink, do middle-aged breakdancing moves, even sing old R&B and hip-hop songs.

We had a great time that night, and when the DJ at Pacha NYC found out that Mel was in the house, he played "White Lines (Don't Don't Do It)." Mel's girlfriend really went buck wild when they played it. She did a headstand on the dance floor and her wig flew off. As the wig went flying, some random Korean dude grabbed it and put it on and started dancing with it on his head. We were howling, and so was Mel.

My New York crew, "The Vipers," and me.

In late 2007, I decided that we'd record my next DVD in New York at Madison Square Garden. This time, my brother and I decided that we'd go it alone and finance the entire production ourselves. Unlike our *Outsourced* experience, I was finally the one deciding when and where I'd record my special. I decided that Jigar Talati would direct the special. Jig was primarily a documentary filmmaker and had never shot a live performance with six cameras before. That didn't matter to me—he knew the material and he knew me, and he did a great job.

The Saturday night show sold out fairly quickly, so we added another one on Friday. The plan was to record both nights, which is normal when you're recording a special—you catch different things on each show and sometimes some bits work better on one show versus the other. You can also do more coverage of the audience and different cutaways between them and yourself. At the end of it all, you edit back and forth between the best of both shows so that it looks like one continuous performance.

However, on Friday afternoon I got a call from my friend and DJ Starting-from-Scratch, who, along with Spinbad, was my other DJ on the show that weekend. I've known him for almost twenty years. He lived in Brampton, just a few kilometres from where I grew up. The depth of his musical knowledge is astounding and his ability to go from playing Fleetwood Mac to Biggie to Frankie Knuckles all in one set is an amazing thing to hear. When he lived at his mom's house near Kennedy Road, he had taken over the entire basement with his thousand records. They lined all four walls, from floor to ceiling, and he had organized them alphabetically and by genre—much the same way that music is now organized on Serato. Anyway, when he called, he was freaking out about my brother and how he had heard from one of my security guys that my brother had said something about his mom. Scratch told me that he wasn't going to be on the show and wouldn't go anywhere where my brother was. My security had spoken out of turn and had misquoted my brother. The drama was the last thing I needed that day. I got on the phone with him and asked him what happened. He knew right away that he'd said the wrong thing. And now, on the first day of recording my special in the most important city in the world, I had lost one of my DJs—who wasn't just a DJ, but a good friend—and it was caused by some unnecessary tongues flapping.

This wasn't the first time we'd had an issue with this particular security guy saying the wrong thing to someone and creating problems for the entire crew, so I flipped out on him and fired him—for the second time in two years. I made it clear that he was not to be in the theatre at any point over the next two days. There was no excuse for this. All of these guys, my security guards Ray Ray and Shake, my DJs Spin, Scratch and Pick, my brother—they all knew how high the stakes were for me that weekend. There's no room for fucking around when you play New York. My brother would have to make amends with Scratch immediately, and he did. I couldn't have been more disappointed in my crew for letting me down like that.

A.G. White, my old friend from New York, was my opener that night. A.G. is one of those guys you meet when you're on the road and you can't help but like him. He's a classic New Yorker who grew up in Brooklyn and was a fellow hip-hop head and always comes with respect and old-school manners that only New Yorkers have.

Although he was nervous as hell, A.G. did a great job with the audience, with lots of local shout-outs and references. But when I took the stage, it felt off. It was February, and it had been pouring rain all day. The audience was tired, as big-city audiences often are on a Friday night after a long work week, and the rainy day didn't help. The energy in the room that night was . . . lacking.

I had decided to wear a white blazer and jeans for the show. My brother and Jig warned me that a white blazer was going to mess up the lighting and the shot, but because of all the drama earlier, there was no way they were going to get into a big thing with me about it. They had no choice but to let it ride.

Even though I'd honed this act across Canada and around the world in 2007 and had chosen these two nights to record it, I was nowhere near as tight as I should have been on that first show. I was nervous and the day's drama had really pissed me off, and I'm not so good at hiding my emotions. My concentration was thrown and my bits were going too long. I was meandering through some of them. I knew that that night's set was unusable. All my guys could see that I was off too. I knew I'd have to knock it out of the park the next night. There was no room for error. I'd also need to ditch that white jacket. When you watch *Red, White and Brown*, you can see the better parts of the Friday show in the bonus features—"The White Jacket Bootleg."

By the end of that night, I was exhausted and just crashed at the hotel. The next day, I went shopping. I bought a black shirt from D&G as well as jeans and sneakers from Gucci. When I got to Madison Square Garden on Saturday night, the whole vibe was different. I was more relaxed, and so was everyone else. It was all very positive backstage. Jigar and my brother had tweaked all the lighting and technical issues that afternoon, and they were feeling good too. From the moment Melle Mel introduced me from offstage, I was on. My back was up against the wall, and I came out swinging. The audience was on fire, right there with me.

One of the first things I really did notice was "the kid" who was there in the audience with his dad. If you watch the DVD, you'll see the one I mean. I make a joke about how the kid's really going to learn "some new shit" that night. Since that show, I've actually met "the kid," Nicholas, and his dad, Dean, at one of my shows in Jersey. And just so people know, Nicholas came away from that Madison Square Garden show unscarred. There were some bits that still worked better on the Friday show, so we put those into the bonus features on the DVD. Looking back, I've noticed that I swore a lot in the Saturday night show. I don't know why I did, and really wish I hadn't.

Me with "the kid," Nicholas, and his father, Dean.

In the end, we licensed broadcast rights to *Red, White and Brown* to Showtime, with a second licence to Comedy Central. We sold over 100,000 copies of the DVD across Canada. Producing *Red, White and Brown* myself turned out to be a great business and creative decision.

When I first came through New York for my show at the Beacon, and then when I came back for the Madison Square Garden show, my agents pitched me to be a guest on *The Late Show with David Letterman*. The producers told them that my material was "too broad" and that they weren't interested in having me on. I've never been sure what "too broad" means. When I'm performing, I'm playing for everyone, not just the comics at the back of the room. I'm there for the audience. That's

You don't play New York to make money. You play New York because it's New York.

my job—to make the audience laugh. I didn't take it personally, but I did think it was funny that they found me "too broad."

There's a saying in the industry that you don't play New York to make money. You play New York because it's New York. On January 29 and 30, 2010, I returned to the city. I could have gone back to Madison Square Garden, but this time I chose to do the shows at Radio City Music Hall. New York has so many historic clubs and theatres to choose from, and I just felt that Radio City sounded pretty cool!

The energy and excitement surrounding a New York show is unlike that of any other city, other than perhaps my shows in Toronto. The more prestigious the venue, the more the tickets cost. Radio City Music Hall is no exception. The room itself is cavernous and absolutely beautiful. The backstage space actually has a camel-holding area for the camels and other livestock that appear in their annual Christmas spectacular. There are three floors of dressing rooms to accommodate the eighty Rockettes that the building is famous for.

January, 2010.

I usually start off every year by playing club dates before I start playing larger venues. I think of it as training camp. Since I hate cold weather, I like to start the year with gigs in Florida. But in January 2010, Florida had one of its coldest winters in history—boy, did my plan backfire. Over the course of playing the improv clubs in Miami, West Palm Beach and Tampa, I picked up a cold. My flight from Tampa was delayed for over ten hours and I was anxious to get the hell out of there and into New York. I bit the bullet and hired a private jet, which is something that I've done before, but not something that I do lightly. It still feels like I'm being extravagant.

I was coming off that cold when I got to New York. My mom and her neighbour Sunita flew in to see me. On Wednesday night, we went out for dinner with the Vipers and around eleven-thirty, while we were driving Mom and her friend around Manhattan to show them the city, Mom said, "Let's go to Atlantic City!" I can't say no to my mom, and she can't say no to a casino, even one that's 150 miles away. So, even though I'd been awake since six-thirty in the morning, *and* I was sick *and* I had two big shows coming up in less than forty-eight hours *and* we were already in one of the greatest cities in the world *AND* I should know better, I said, "Okay, Mom."

Mama and me in Atlantic City.

Two hours later, we arrived at the Borgata Casino in Atlantic City. Mom lost a few hundred bucks and then we returned to Manhattan. I got to bed at around 6:30 A.M. and crashed out.

Like the Madison Square Garden shows, my Friday-night show at Radio City Music Hall wasn't as strong as I would have liked. Michael Bublé was in town doing *Saturday Night Live*, and he came to the show. I was really happy to see him. We met when I was hosting the Juno Awards in 2008 and we hit it off. Like me, he comes from a very modest working-class background. Before the show, he came backstage and had a nice casual dinner in the general dining area where all of the crew guys eat. No fanfare, no fuss, just a couple of working-class Canadian guys having dinner in New York City.

In addition to having Bublé at the Friday show, the mayor of Brampton, Susan Fennell, was there too. We also had a veritable who's who of my hip-hop heroes at those shows: DJ Premier, Masta Ace, Freddie Foxxx (a.k.a. Bumpy Knuckles), Skoob (Das EFX), Vinnie (from Naughty by Nature), Pharoahe Monch, DJ Riz, Grandmaster Kaz, Greg Nice, Marco Polo, Torae and Craig G, as well as Ali Leroy and Terry

New York has never let me down, and having any kind of success there is different from having success anywhere else in the world.

Crews from *Everybody Hates Chris* and Opie from *The Opie and Anthony Show*. We even had Mark Teixeira from the New York Yankees there. Having a Yankee at your show in New York is like having royalty. Mark was a really nice, down-to-earth guy, and he came with his wife and family. Mark's also the cousin of my L.A. manager, Paul Canterna. When I introduced Mark to Melle Mel, Mel was impressed. He went from being Melle Mel of Grandmaster Flash and the Furious Five to a regular New Yorker in awe of meeting a real live New York Yankee.

My opener at these shows was a very funny comic named Owen Smith. Owen had opened for me a few times on some of my club dates and had been giving me some acting and auditioning advice. His advice in these two areas was invaluable and led to a career-changing opportunity, which I'll tell you about later. His entire family of about twenty or so people, including his mom, were at the shows, and he was dressed sharp. He went out there and totally killed on both nights.

Once again, Saturday night's show was much better than Friday's. I was giddy and downright silly when I got on stage that night. I was making myself laugh. I couldn't have asked for a better mix of people in the front rows. It was a multicultural Noah's Ark—Filipinos, Latinos, Indians, Italians, Arabs . . . you name it. I was happy with the show and as far as I could tell, so was the audience.

New York has never let me down, and having any kind of success there is different from having success anywhere else in the world. It really does make you feel like if you can make it there, you'll make it anywhere. No matter what happens to my career in the future, I'll always be able to look back and know that for a few hours over the course of a few nights, I was king of the hill and the top of the heap.

CHAPTER 11

L.A. TIMES

IF YOU'VE ever seen my MTV *Diary* episode, you know that I bought my first house in L.A. in the Hollywood Hills from a former porn star. I moved to Los Angeles in February 2006, almost ten years after my first trip there.

When I step back and read these first two sentences, they seem a bit surreal to me. As much as I had always dreamed of stringing these words together, never did I think they would ever come true. If America is some fantasy place that all of us growing up in Canada watch on TV, then Los Angeles is where the fantasy begins.

Shortly after moving into that house in L.A., I went back to my old townhouse in Woodbridge. Despite having moved out, my old bedroom was exactly how I'd left it—same pile of clothes on the floor, same dresser, bedding, pictures . . . everything. After a few days of being back, I woke up one afternoon and looked around my room. I sat there staring at everything, then started asking myself if all that L.A. stuff was real. Was L.A. all a dream and Woodbridge the reality? It took a few seconds for it to sink in, but L.A. *was* real. I really did own a house there. I had friends and another life there too. I'd really done it.

As a kid in the '70s, watching TV with my parents, we'd watch *The Brady Bunch, The Love Boat, Fantasy Island, Charlie's Angels, Three's Company, CHiPs, Emergency!* . . . and the list goes on. Almost all of those shows were set in Los Angeles. The people on those shows had blond hair, great smiles, funky clothes, convertible sports cars—and it was always, always sunny. Aesthetically, it was very pleasing to me.

Los Angeles was a world away from Brampton. We were ethnic, with dark hair and dark eyes. The closest we got to seeing people who looked somewhat like us on television was Erik Estrada on *CHiPs*, or Ricardo Montalban on *Fantasy Island*—and both of them were Latino. As a kid, I was convinced that Erik Estrada was Indian, like me. To this day, I have suspicions about that guy . . .

In November 1996 I flew down to L.A. The city looked exactly like I thought it would—sunny, clean and downright glamorous. The only misconception that I had was that gangs would be everywhere and that

I shouldn't wear red or blue. (I may have watched *Boyz n the Hood, Colors, American Me* and *Menace II Society* one too many times in the early '90s.) I'm not saying there are no gangs in L.A., but they're so localized that you can avoid them.

Somehow during that trip, we got invited to Russell Simmons' place for a party. The invite was a cigar with a Def Jam wrapper around it. In order to get to Simmons' mansion, you had to go this hotel in Beverly Hills, where a limo picked you up and took you to the mansion. The dance floor was outside, on the tennis court. Kid Capri DJed and everybody was at that party: Brian McKnight, Kellie Williams (*Family Matters*), Ronnie DeVoe, Ricky Bell, Tiny Lister, Keenen Ivory Wayans, all the Def Jam comedians . . . and me, the unknown comic. I was pretty much invisible at that party, but I didn't mind; I was at a party at Russell Simmons' mansion in Hollywood on my very first visit to L.A.! I didn't perform anywhere; I just hung out for a few days. Let's just say I got a feel for a world that no longer seemed so far away.

Basically, he was going to "make me a star."

In 1997, I landed my first management deal, with Inner City Management, which was owned by Chuck and Percy Sutton. They'd seen me at Just for Laughs and taken me on. I flew out to L.A. for two shows and stayed at the Travelodge on Sunset Boulevard. Nobody of any importance attended. The people I did meet really liked my business card . . . which I guess says something about how good my act was.

I went back in 2004 while on the Gurus of Comedy tour, and I met this film producer named Deepak Nayar. He saw the show and invited me out to dinner with him on Melrose. He'd produced a bunch of TV shows and was one of the producers of the film *Bend It Like Beckham*. He wanted me to sign a deal with him and his production company. Basically, he was going to "make me a star." I was going to live in his guest house and he was going to take me around to all the networks and studios and launch my career.

I'll be honest with you—it sounded pretty cool. And like most Indians, this guy was a pretty convincing talker. When I got back to Toronto, he sent me a contract. Our agreement would last seven years, and we'd be 50/50 partners. He would get 50 per cent of whatever I made! Now, I don't claim to be a smart guy, but seriously? Needless to say, I didn't sign.

On that same trip, the producer of the Gurus tour, Piyush Dinker Pandya, introduced me to a young agent named Ashwin Rajan from United Talent Agency. Before setting up the meeting, Piyush asked me, "If I set you up with this guy and something comes from it, what will you do for me?" Fucking Indians—always trying to work an angle.

I answered him, "Um . . . nothing."

Nothing came of the meeting, but Ashwin did mention me to his boss at UTA, who responded, "An Indian comic? I don't get it." That guy who "didn't get it" is now part of my team of agents at CAA!

After my showcase gigs in L.A. in 2005, I got my first holding deal, in which a studio or production company puts a bunch of money down to "hold" you to develop a project with them (and to keep you from developing a project somewhere else). The deal was with the production company Werner/Gold/Miller, with Warner Brothers as the studio.

Tom Werner was the former producing partner of Marcy Carsey—as in Carsey-Werner, as in *The Cosby Show, Roseanne, A Different World, 3rd Rock from the Sun* . . . and the list goes on. Tom had just formed a new production company with super-managers Eric Gold and Jimmy Miller. Eric and Jimmy managed everyone from Jim Carrey to Vince Vaughn and Will Ferrell. All of these guys were serious heavy hitters.

Once we locked in our deal, we moved ahead with developing a sitcom for me. My brother and I hadn't yet been working together for five months when this all started. We were green as green could be and had never been through the development process before.

The first thing you need to develop a show is a writer. Tom Werner liked a young, fellow Harvard alumnus named Tom Brady, and we liked him too. It was now coming up on September, which is late for pitching a show to a network. Everybody had an idea of what the show should be—Eric wanted a workplace comedy; Jimmy wanted something more family focused; Tom wanted to see something in the middle. And me? I just sat back and let them do their thing. I tried to be as cooperative as possible. When you get into a room with shooters like these guys, you need to acknowledge that *theirs* is bigger than *yours*, especially back in '05. (Mine's grown quite a bit since then.)

Whatever misgivings I had about the actual concept, I kept to myself—including the use of "Somebody Gonna Get a-Hurt Real Bad" as a character tagline and the use of other bits of mine in the show. It's not that I didn't want to use this stuff; it just seemed a little forced. But what did I know? By mid-October we had decided the show would be about a multicultural, mega car dealership in the San Fernando Valley.

My brother and I were flying back and forth from Toronto to L.A. for the studio and writer meetings. We stayed at the Hyatt on Sunset and had started working with Paul Canterna at Seven Summits Pictures and Management as an L.A. manager. Paul, or Paully Walnuts, as I call him, comes from a very Catholic working-class family in the small town of Latrobe, Pennsylvania. He's honest and down to earth and not very "L.A." at all, which was important to me. He works hard for me and has become a good and trusted friend.

The show was going to be called *Those People*, and once the script was done we scrambled to pitch it to the networks. Before you actually pitch a show, you get together with everyone involved and work out who's going to say what and when. I have to admit that I thought the show was a bit contrived—we had an African guy, a Latina, my very Indian parents, a redneck mechanic, an Asian guy and a WASPy dealership owner. The concept wasn't great, and I think we knew it.

Still, everyone wanted to hear the pitch from Tom Werner's new company—ABC, CBS, NBC, Fox and the WB. The only network that didn't pass after the pitches was Fox. But they weren't entirely convinced and wanted a table read before they would decide whether they'd order a pilot. For the read, we hired a comedian friend of mine, Godfrey, to play the Nigerian car salesman, Boomie Moshoeshoe, as well as Gerry

Bednob as my dad and Shelley Malil as my brother. Gerry and Shelley were both in *The 40-Year-Old Virgin*. Tom Werner pulled in a favour and got Kurtwood Smith from *That 70's Show* to play the dealership manager for the read.

We did the table read at a screening room at Fox on February 15, 2006. Everyone did their best to make it funny, but the read was flat, and by that afternoon we'd received word that Fox had passed on the show. I got the balance of my payment for the holding deal and moved on.

In the midst of trying to get my first sitcom off the ground, I moved into my new house in the Hills, bought a year-old Porsche Cayenne Turbo, taped my first U.S. stand-up special, wrapped up my first solo Canadian tour, signed with CAA for representation, secured a great lawyer, Dale de la Torre, and even hired a business manager to look after all of my financial matters. Brandi and Fred from my business management company helped me get my financial act together by ensuring that all of my taxes were taken care of properly. As much as I hate paying taxes, Brandi and Fred make sure they're always paid and then some. There's enough cautionary tales in this business regarding unpaid taxes, and I don't want to become a character in one of them.

As I got settled into L.A., I spent a lot of time hanging out with comedian Yoshi Obayashi and the Mexican-Jewish brothers Isaac and Jacob Giron. Yoshi is Korean, but was raised as Japanese. He indexes porn DVDs as his day job. (When his bosses are pissed off with him, they make him index tranny porn.) Yoshi and his brother were born in Japan, where they lived until he was eleven. When his mom and dad divorced, his mom took the two boys and dumped them with his cousins in Washington State. His cousins only spoke broken English and Korean, and Yoshi and his brother spoke only Japanese. It was at this time that his mom decided to let them

Hanging out with Yoshi.

know that they *weren't* actually Japanese, but Korean. Now, this might not seem like a big deal to most of us, but there's a long history of animosity between the two peoples. To add insult to injury, Yoshi and his brother would get beaten up in their newly adopted navy town in Washington State, because the locals thought they were Japanese. Their mother returned for the boys, and they ultimately became legal citizens under Reagan's immigration amnesty in 1986.

Even though Yoshi's been in the country since he was eleven, he still has the thickest Japanese accent I've ever heard. His brother, on the other hand, has no accent whatsoever. In the fall of 2003, just three weeks after his father killed himself in Japan, Yoshi got a terrible call that his cousin had killed himself in Seattle.

He grabbed his knapsack and some clothes and went straight to the airport. When he put his knapsack through the security scanner, the alarms went off and the police were called. They opened up the knapsack to find a collapsible iron baton—which is illegal not just to fly with but to carry as a concealed weapon in general. Yoshi forgot that he had it with him. He'd carried it for protection since his days as a video store clerk in Seattle, when he'd get hassled late at night while working at the store. Security was on high alert that day at the airport—it was September 11, 2003—and they weren't taking any chances.

Yoshi was arrested and taken to L.A. County prison. While waiting to be processed, he was held with his hands cuffed behind him in a holding cell. As he sat there, he started wondering if he'd be able to lift his cuffed hands from behind his back to in front of him, just like he'd seen in the movies. Yoshi's a very slim, fit guy and he was able to slip his arms under his hips and legs and put his hands on his lap. As soon as he did that, he realized that this might not be a good idea. The guard might think he was trying to escape or something, so he decided to return to his original position with his hands behind his back. With his cuffed arms out in front of him, he put one leg through and was about to put the other leg through, when the guard walked in on him. He spent the rest of the night with one arm raised in the air, cuffed to a bar above his head. By the time the police processed him, it was Friday, and he remained in jail for another four days.

I put Yoshi on a bunch of my shows in 2006, including opening for me in Australia. I even put him on a couple of my Canadian dates. Yoshi did some really edgy material, which I know offended a few people at some of my shows. He actually seemed to enjoy watching the audience turn on him. I ultimately stopped putting him on as an opener because I felt that he wasn't taking his craft as a stand-up as seriously as I felt that he should. Nevertheless, Yoshi became a trusted friend to me in those early L.A. days and could always be counted on to look after my house for me when I was travelling and taking care of anything that I needed—including an endless supply of adult DVDs.

By now, my good friend Angelo Tsarouchas had also moved to L.A., and it was good to have him there. He had just gotten his papers and wanted to focus on acting in the States. Ang opened for me when we taped *Outsourced* in San Francisco. We both started getting spots at the Laugh Factory, which was close to my new house and became *my* club in L.A. But this wasn't just any club. On any given night, you could drop by and do a set, and you'd be on shows with guys like Dane Cook, Dom Irerra, Dave Chappelle, Bobby Lee, Dave Attell—even Chris Rock and Eddie Murphy would drop by just to do a set. Jamie, the club's owner, is well known in the comedy world and was really good to me early on. He's the kind of owner who won't let just anyone take the stage at his club, and I was honoured that he'd let me be part of this group of guys.

My good friend Angelo and me.

I'd become a bit of an urban myth—the Indian guy from Canada who was selling out two- and three-thousand-seat theatres across the States and internationally.

Remember that none of these guys really knew me. I'd become a bit of an urban myth—the Indian guy from Canada who was selling out two- and three-thousand-seat theatres across the States and internationally. It took some time, but after several months of just doing walk-ons, these other comics started to get to know me. They'd call and invite me to do other shows, and I was happy to go. I also started doing spots at the Melrose Improv. I'd made friends with some of the Latino comics, and they'd invite me to be on their shows.

The Latino shows in L.A. have like fourteen comics in a row, and sometimes I'd be the last guy up. You look out into the audience and there's these hard-looking Mexican kids, their arms, necks and sometimes their faces all tatted up. Growing up in Canada, there really weren't any Mexicans around, or Latinos in general, so I didn't really know their community or their culture. It was intimidating at first, and I wasn't sure how these guys were going to take to my stuff. Fortunately, they were right there with me, and as I did more and more of those nights, they'd come up to me after the shows and give me props on my set. (*Whew!*)

I should mention that I've really come to love Mexicans. Once I moved to L.A., I started to get a better understanding of their culture. They are the hardest-working people around. They love their families and always come with respect. I really believe that the entire state of California would come to a grinding halt if it weren't for them. Almost every valet in L.A. is Mexican, and for me, it's more important for me to be friends with the valet of a restaurant than with the manager or maître d'. It's not like the valets can do anything for me, it's just that I identify with them more than I do with anyone else. Hell, if it weren't for pure luck, I'd probably be one of them!

I don't see these guys as taking jobs away from hard-working Americans; they're usually doing jobs that Americans just don't want to do anymore. I can't help but look at them and see my dad or my mom when they first came to Canada: a little scared, a little poor, but they're there for a better life and many of them have sacrificed everything for their shot at it.

My assistant in L.A. is Mexican. Eddie's a great kid. He takes good care of me and my family when we're in town. He's also ridiculously positive and makes me laugh with his "go team" attitude.

In the fall of 2006, I was back to work on another sitcom opportunity. This time, there was no holding deal. We were working with Doug Liman's company, Dutch Oven, trying to develop a show for me. Doug had seen me perform at the Aspen Comedy Arts Festival earlier in the year. He came to the show with Vince Vaughn, Jennifer Aniston and Jon Favreau. They all arrived late and were seated a few rows back from the stage. And even though I was up there doing my thing, everyone in the place just stopped when they came in and watched them sit down. At the time, Vaughn and Aniston were *the* hot Hollywood couple. When I looked out into the audience, all I could see were their faces. They were the biggest stars I'd seen to that point, and I was completely starstruck. Thing was, it didn't look like they were laughing, and it was freaking me out! I don't think I had a great set that night.

Anyway, Doug Liman's company had a deal with NBC and was looking to develop more television and thought that we could do something together. They brought in the writing team of Jim and Steve Armogida, these two American brothers who had been working on the British show *My Family*. They lived in London and had a good, English sensibility about them, which meant that they got my material and understood South Asians, since there are *soooo* many of them in England. They also reminded me of my brother and me; we really liked them. Unfortunately, we were once again getting started late in the game and the show never came together.

At the same time as we were trying to develop this project, I was being courted by Simon Fuller, the creator of *American Idol* (well, all the Idol shows, originating with *Pop Idol* in the UK). He had come to my L.A. show at the Wiltern Theatre that fall with my agent. (To hear my agent tell it, he was the one who specifically invited Fuller to the show. To hear Simon tell it, they were out at dinner and my agent told him he had to go to a show and Simon decided to come along.) Anyway, he wanted to develop a "global talk show," and with his record of success, there was no reason to think that we couldn't do something great together. Unfortunately, Simon was so busy with *Idol* and the Beckhams that we couldn't really get the project off the ground. Frankly, it was pretty cool just to know him. He was very nice to me and even introduced me to Victoria Beckham at his office when I was there one day.

In July 2007, we were scheduled for a general meeting at Fox. The studio and TV execs had been at my show at Just for Laughs earlier in the month and wanted to get together with me when I got back to L.A.

The Fox execs were all really cool, and we were sitting around shooting the shit with them when the president of the network joined the meeting. He popped in to hear what we were talking about and asked me what, if any, projects I wanted to develop. My brother had written a treatment for a show that was basically about our family ten years earlier—an Anglo-Indian working-class family, where the dad was recently retired and the mom worked in a K-mart cafeteria. My character was a struggling comic and my older brother had a successful career. Although this wasn't a formal pitch meeting, Kevin Reilly, the president of entertainment of Fox Broadcasting, loved the idea and "bought it in the room," as they say.

We were back in development again. Once again, we needed to find a writer for what we called *The Russell Peters Show*, and not just a writer, a showrunner—a guy who runs the entire show, from the writers to the cast, production staff, budgets and everything else. Showrunners are as important as the stars. They can make or break a show, and every network has a list of guys who are "approved."

Our pick for showrunner was Jim Hope. He was a former writer on *The George Lopez Show*, and my brother introduced me to him at the Hermosa Beach Comedy Club. Jim was a white guy who was a former stand-up comic. He grew up in a working-class family in East L.A. and was married to a black woman. He now lived in Orange County (the O.C.) in a Korean neighbourhood. He really understood everything that I was about. A lot of the people I've met in L.A. come from pretty well-off families, which means that getting a writer who understands the struggles of the working class is really hard to do. Unfortunately, Jim wasn't a network-approved showrunner, so we had to go with someone else.

My agents set up a series of meetings with at least a dozen writers who were approved by the network. During the all-day meetings, held at CAA, I decided to wear a giant, one-inch-thick, fake gold chain over my T-shirt. Why? you might ask. I wanted a writer who could look beyond the surface.

I'll admit I wasn't at my best that day and sat there doodling as the writers came in to meet with me, my brother and Paully. My brother would nudge me under the table to pay attention when he thought I had "gone to the happy place." But the thing about me is that even when it looks like I'm not listening, I am. I know I should be sitting pretty and looking the corporate part, but that doesn't mean I'm not paying attention. Sometimes that pisses people off. I know I pissed off some of the writers that day. One guy even told my agent that before meeting me that he was a fan. After the meeting, he couldn't stand me.

Looking back, I was completely wrong-headed in these meetings. For you kids out there, you should know that there's an art to securing a writer. You have to seduce them. I was sitting there thinking that I was doing them a favour—meanwhile, these guys have tons of opportunities, especially if they're known guys. They make as much as (and sometimes more than) the leads in the shows they write. Think of guys like Larry David from *Seinfeld* or Phil Rosenthal from *Everybody Loves Raymond*. They were the showrunners and creators. They're worth hundreds of millions of dollars.

After these meetings, we made a shortlist of guys that we felt we could work with and who were still interested in working with us. Jim Hope was still my main choice, and we pushed hard for him, but the network exec assigned to my show wasn't hearing it. They liked someone else, a guy named Ben Wexler, and to be honest, I couldn't even remember which guy he was after our first meeting.

Because the network was very hot on this guy, we decided to move ahead with him. The short version of this story is that, as we started working on the pilot script, the writers' strike started. By the time the strike ended on February 12, 2008, the network wanted a script within ten days. Ben had adhered to the "pens down" rule that the strike mandated. But we weren't very happy with the script he submitted to the network. He was having trouble understanding the nuances of our working-class family and he wasn't prepared to make any changes to the script.

Fox passed on the show. If you ever wonder why I don't get too hyped up on anything in Hollywood, it's because of having gone through things like this. I hate being disappointed and don't believe that anything is going to happen until *after* it's happened.

During all of this, I was still going out on auditions for different television guest-starring roles as well as roles in movies. None of these auditions went very well. I just wasn't good at auditioning. My live shows were getting bigger and bigger, and I was making more and more money on the road. It was kind of tough to go from that part of my life to being in a waiting room with a bunch of guys who either looked like me or were the usual group of stand-up comics that I knew. It was funny (or not so funny) to watch the Korean comedian Ken Jeong, a.k.a. Dr. Ken, get every role that I also read for: the barista in an episode of *Entourage*, the gynecologist in *Knocked Up*, and a bunch of other movies that came out in 2007 and 2008.

I was always asked to play characters with an "Indian accent," and I kept turning those roles down—much to my agents' annoyance. As one of my agents, who's actually an Indian guy, told me, "Look, everybody has to do these roles at some point." Not me. I may have fun with the accent in my act, but I didn't want to play an ongoing stereotype in these TV shows and movies I was auditioning for. When I would read the script, I'd never see any reason for the characters to have an accent. It just didn't make sense.

After getting increasingly fed up with being just another face from CAA's roster, I had Paully specifically ask whether I'd been requested for auditions by the producers or casting agents. If I was just going to be another guy reading, then I wasn't going to audition. Maybe I sound like an asshole here, but what's the point of being just another face in the room? I was sucking at it and would put in a minimal amount of effort because I didn't want to deal with the rejection. If I didn't try, I didn't fail.

In January of 2009, I was invited to a meeting with the Simmons Lathan Media Group in L.A. This is the company owned by Russell Simmons and Stan Lathan—two media legends. They wanted to talk about developing a show for me—maybe a talk show, maybe a variety show, maybe a sitcom. Initially, we were thinking about a talk show, but then we heard that George Lopez was going to develop a late-night talk show, so that idea was canned.

Next, we discussed me hosting a new stand-up series for them, featuring multi-ethnic comics. That would have been *okay*, but I had already done that with *Comics Without Borders*, for Showtime. Eventually, we moved away from the stand-up series and came around to getting a sitcom off the ground. Kim Fleary, one of the execs at Simmons Lathan, used to work at ABC and had worked with writer and showrunner Bruce Helford. Bruce had co-created *The Drew Carey*

Show as well as *The Norm Show, Wanda at Large* and *The George Lopez Show*, among others, and came from a working-class background in Chicago. We met with Bruce and really liked him. I'd finally moved up the food chain to working with an A-list showrunner. I was excited.

I had Bruce Helford and Russell Simmons behind me. Bruce had this English sitcom that he wanted to develop for the States, with me as the lead. As he worked on that, we also kicked around other ideas for a show. We all liked the traditional three-camera sitcoms (like *Friends* and *The Drew Carey Show*, among others) versus the current trend towards one-camera sitcoms (*The Office, Modern Family, 30 Rock*). By October 2009, Bruce wasn't able to make any progress with securing the rights to the British series and didn't feel that a three-camera series would work at the time. *Modern Family* (I love that show) had started on ABC and became an immediate hit, which he interpreted as a sign that the networks would continue with the one-camera format. This meant that by October 2009, I was once again sitcom-less.

I ended up setting a new attendance record of almost seven thousand people.

So back to the stage I went. Over the past two years, I've played two big shows in L.A., both of them at the Nokia Theatre. My first show at the Nokia was in February 2008. The theatre was only open a few months at that time, and I ended up setting a new attendance record of almost seven thousand people. The week before the Nokia date, I was booked on *The Tonight Show* with Jay Leno. Being on *The Tonight Show* is something all comics dream of. It's also one of those things that people ask you about—"Oh, you're a comedian? Have you ever been on *The Tonight Show*?" In a way, it validates you, because everybody knows the show.

Before you can do stand-up on *The Tonight Show*, you need to run your set past the stand-up producers—Bob Read and Ross Mark. We ran through the set at the Hermosa Beach Comedy and Magic Club, and it went well. I was given some notes afterwards. The one thing that they insisted on is that my set be "joke, joke, joke, joke." The pace has got to be fast. Their focus, as on all TV shows, is ratings. If you're going too slowly, the network may lose viewers—not good.

But I'm a storyteller. I don't do "joke, joke, joke, joke," so I had to adjust my style a bit for the show. Next, I did a pre-interview. The producers run through things that Jay may ask you, and you have a chance to prepare good answers. Everything went well in the run-through, and Bob and Ross, who are both really good guys, were happy with my set.

A few days later, I was at *The Tonight Show*. Jay came by my dressing room to say hi and see what I was up to. He's a stand-up, so he knew I'd be a bit nervous. He was really supportive and cool with me. Also on the show that night was singer and actress Kristin Chenoweth, who was a great guest and really loosened up the show before I came on and did my thing. I moved through my set quickly, as requested, and it went really well. I even included Kevin Eubanks (Jay's bandleader) as part of one of the bits. The only thing that threw me off was a Canadian fan in the audience who yelled out during my set. Not a big deal, though.

After I wrapped my set, Jay invited me over to the desk. I sat down and somehow immediately began flirting with Kristin. Jay was great and we went through all of the questions comfortably—except for one. Jay asked me if I liked hockey—a question all Canadians in L.A. get asked. In the pre-interview I had answered that I liked boxing instead of hockey, and that was supposed to lead to a joke—a joke that to this day, I can't even remember. So Jay asked me if I liked hockey, and I simply answered, "No." That was it. I had no comeback.

Jay paused for a second and then repeated, "So you don't like hockey?"

"Nah, nope," I replied.

He moved on, and between flirting with Kristin and joking around with Jay, things went well. After the show was over, one of the producers mentioned that I didn't answer the hockey question the way we'd discussed in the pre-interview. I was like, "I forgot." Sometimes, that's just the way it goes.

When we released *Red, White and Brown* in the States in the fall of 2008, my agents tried to get me back on *The Tonight Show*. They said that they'd love to have me on for stand-up, but that I wouldn't be able to do panel. "Huh? I thought it went pretty well last time."

Turns out that by not answering the hockey question properly, I had "gone off script." Because of that, I wouldn't be invited back to panel. There was nothing anyone could do.

Sometimes, when you're disappointed, you've got to just say fuck it. I ended up doing *The Late Late Show with Craig Ferguson* instead to promote the DVD release—and doing Craig's show meant that I couldn't do Jay's show or even *Jimmy Kimmel Live*. All these shows compete for guests, and if you appear on one, you can't do the other. I was a huge fan of Craig's movie *The Big Tease*. Craig's a very funny guy and the show's very relaxed, so we had a good time together.

This past year I did *Lopez Tonight* to tie in with my Nokia show. George has a huge studio audience and probably the most hyped-up crowd in late night. I personally think the set and the show look wicked, both on TV and when you're in the studio. There was no screening of my set beforehand. We just gave the producers an idea of what I was going to do. As part of my pre-interview, we discussed the fact that I liked to roller-skate, so they suggested that I bring my skates with me. We'd do a quick shot of me roller-skating backstage for one of the bumpers.

Now, I consider myself a pretty good skater—I've been doing it for thirty years. I was actually feeling like a bit of a show-off. But . . . the floor backstage at *Lopez* is made of Astroturf, of all things. When the crew was ready to shoot the bumper, I stepped out of my dressing room and my skates got caught on the Astroturf. I fell flat. All of the hot producer chicks were there, and I was embarrassed as shit. I pulled myself up and regained my composure and they did a shot of me gliding effortlessly across the Astroturf.

When I got on stage to do my set, I had to really go for it because George's intro wasn't very hype. But that's okay. The audience was great and my set went well. When George and I sat down, we talked about my recent dinner with the king of Jordan, and I mentioned that he served us alcohol. The king wasn't drinking, but that didn't matter. I wish that part had been edited out, because it upset some Muslims who felt that the king shouldn't be offering alcohol since it's prohibited by the Qur'an. It wasn't like my Muslim and Arab fans turned on me, but I don't aim to offend people's religion.

Me and Lopez, then and now, 2000 and 2010 (*Lopez Tonight*).

I also realized that, while telling the story of how the king punked me, I said that his guards had Uzis—which of course is a gun that no Arab country would use because they're made in Israel. Sorry, guys. The Uzi is the only machine-gun name I know.

The day after I did Lopez's show, I appeared on a fundraiser he was having for Haitian earthquake relief. I walked into the greenroom at the Nokia Theatre and everyone was there—Sam Jackson,

Magic Johnson, Olden Polynice, Don Cheadle, Andy Garcia, Larry David, Los Lobos, Amber Valletta, Ray Romano, Eva Longoria, Slash, George Clinton, Charlie Wilson, Cypress Hill . . . and Cedric the Entertainer. The *only* person who recognized me was Cedric. He was like, "Hey, Russell Peters!"

L.A. is the home of hugely successful celebrities. I'm not trying to name-drop by listing all these players. I just want to give you an idea of where I fit in the grander scheme of things. I may be doing okay, but some of these guys are at a whole other level—and I still get starstruck by many of them.

That night, it was getting late and I was starting to wonder if I was even supposed to perform. Cypress Hill went up and absolutely killed it. I was next. Turns out I was closing the show. The room was still buzzing from Cypress Hill's performance, so I wasn't sure what was going to happen, but somehow that audience was right there with me, and I had a great set.

Many people see me as a celebrity, but I definitely don't think of myself as one.

Many people see me as a celebrity, but I definitely don't think of myself as one. At the end of the day, I'm just a guy who goes onstage and talks about race and culture and maybe throws in a few dick jokes and then goes home. My audiences may have grown from thirty people to thirty thousand, but I don't feel all that different from the way I did ten years ago. I've done a couple of specials, hosted some TV shows and put out two official DVDs. I know that I have a fan base who will support me.

What I never, ever considered was that the stuff I've done would be seen by other performers and real celebrities. That honestly never occurred to me until I met Rebecca Romijn and Jerry O'Connell when I was filming the movie *The Con Artist* (yet to be released). We shot this movie in Toronto and Hamilton in the spring of 2009, and it was done on a pretty low budget. Rebecca was in the movie and so was Rossif Sutherland, who played the lead, as well as his father, Donald.

One day, Rebecca called me into her trailer. She said, "I watched all your stuff when I was pregnant. I'm a really big fan!" I thought she was shitting me. I asked her how she first saw my work. "One of my neighbours put me onto you."

"Who are your neighbours?"

"Angie Harmon and Jason Sehorn." Harmon had seen me on TV when *she* was pregnant and then picked up *Red, White and Brown* and *Outsourced*. During her pregnancy she had torn a disc in her back and was completely bedridden. The only thing that would make her laugh during that time were my specials. She passed the DVDs on to Rebecca during her pregnancy and she loved them, too.

On February 6, Angie, Rebecca, Jason and Jerry all came to my show at Nokia. They seemed sincerely happy to be there. Because they all had kids, this was a big night out for all of them. Afterwards, Jerry O'Connell asked me where I grew up, and I told him, "Brampton."

He replied, "Oh yeah, Brampton."

I was like, "You know Brampton?"

"Sure, it's just north of Mississauga."

It was probably the last thing I was expecting to hear that night.

(From left) Jerry O'Connell, Rebecca Romijn, me, Angie Harmon and Jason Sehorn.

PART FOUR

ON THE

ROAD
ISAF

THE WHOLE WORLD'S MIXING. THERE'S NOTHING YOU CAN DO ABOUT IT.

In about three hundred years, there's not going to be any more white people or black people. Everyone's just going to be beige. And I don't care. I'm already beige.

We're all going to become some sort of hybrid between Chinese and Indian. They're the two largest populations in the world.

And since we're going to mix anyway, why not start mixing now? Ladies: take some chances, sleep around a bit. If you see that Indian comedian that you really want to have sex with, I say go for it! And while we're at it, maybe we should just start mixing races now that would never normally mix, just to see what we'll get, like hooking up a Jamaican with an Italian. They could have little Pastafarians. I'm Indian, I could hook up with a Jew, and we could have little Hinjews. Get a guy from the Philippines with a girl from Holland—Hollapinos. Girl from Cuba with a guy from Iceland—little Icecubes. A French and a Greek—Freek. A German and a Newfie—little Goofies.

It's gonna happen. We might as well help it along.

CHAPTER 12

THAT'S OUR RUSSELL

Could you imagine an all Indian ice hockey team, "THe Toronto Maple Sikhs!" Just think they wouldn't have to wear helmet's, just blue and white turbans. I could just hear the commentary now, from City t.v. with Sureal Joshi, "And here comes Singh down center ice, he passes it to Singh, Singh shoots it over to Singh, Singh shoots at Singh he misses!" "What's this, a fight!? Uh oh! here come the ceremonial daggers!" That's just a recap of tonights game, now for the weather here's Harold Hosaine."

"THANK You Sureal, Well get your golashes ready it's gonna be a wet one thank you goodnight!"

DEAD

MY DAD had a few sayings, and one that has always stuck with me is this: Only a fool makes the same mistake twice. It's true about boxing, and it's true about comedy.

In 1995, I made a joke about a Punjabi hockey team called the Toronto Maple Sikhs. Overall, it was a pretty innocent joke—or so I thought—about how the team wouldn't wear helmets, just blue-and-white turbans. To be honest, I'd only picked the word *Sikh* because it was a one-syllable word that sounded like Leafs. The Toronto Maple *Hindus* just wouldn't have worked at all.

Even though I'd meant the joke without malice, it was taken very, very seriously by some Sikhs. The issue became so heated that I even received death threats over it, and it was at that point that I realized I'd touched a nerve without even intending to do so. I decided to do something about the stir I'd caused, so I got in contact with some elders from the Sikh community in the Toronto area. What I wanted to know from them—from these people for whom I actually had a lot of respect—was whether they felt that I'd done something wrong in my jokes, if I'd truly offended them. My biggest fear was that my audience would misunderstand me, and I wanted to be clear to this community that my comedy has never been about hatred.

So I met with these serious-minded elders from the Sikh community, and in particular a man named T. Sher Singh. After talking with him a while about all sorts of things, it was clear to me that this was a brilliant man and a sweet human being. He was someone I could trust to be fair and open-minded. I put my question to him: "Have I done anything wrong?" And T. Sher Singh reassured me that I had not. Then he went even further. He said that on behalf of his community, he wanted me to know that he didn't consider those who'd issued threats against me to be part of his community—and he was firm on this point. His people are peaceful and law-abiding, he insisted, not hoodlums who issue death threats. And I said, "Cool." I figured I was in the clear. I haven't seen him in years, but he's a brilliant and sweet man.

Shortly after my meeting with these elders, I was at a nightclub called Calypso Hut up in Brampton. I was just standing there when three young guys rolled up on me. I'd already had death threats phoned into my house, so I was feeling a bit nervous when these three Punjabi guys surrounded me. Apart from physically intimidating me, they also launched directly into an attack. They were militant and abusive from their very first words, saying that they'd seen me on TV and that I'd not only better watch what I said but should watch my back as well.

One of the three jabbed me, and without thinking much about it, I aimed an uppercut right at him.

Before I could really see it coming, one of the three jabbed me, and without thinking much about it, I aimed an uppercut right at him. Then I hit another guy with a left hook, shoved the one who was issuing the threats out of the way and ran. I ran straight out of that club and never looked back. These were thugs, not fair fighters, and that's the thing that bothered me the most about them. Just the day before, I'd received a whole education about the Sikhs and their religion, so I knew that these were secular young punks claiming that they were acting in the name of their Sikhism when in fact they were going against everything their faith stood for. I'd never set out to offend a deeply religious person, but these guys were just common, dumb thugs.

Shortly after that, I decided that I didn't want to put myself in that sort of situation ever again. I'm a fighter by nature, but there's nothing enjoyable about self-defence, and there's nothing enjoyable about violence. In the interests of keeping the peace, I chose to never again do jokes with anything that might be interpreted as a religious undercurrent. And I've been true to my word ever since.

This wasn't the last time I was to encounter a backlash over my comedy. I was just beginning to make inroads on TV, and my face was starting to get out there. Before the mid-'90s, there really hadn't been many Indians on TV, and I think my sudden appearance on the scene and the fact that I talk honestly about race and culture made more than a few Indians nervous. We're a proud race, so I can understand that people were caught off guard at first. The funny thing is that I wasn't saying anything that my community felt was outrageous—it's just that I'd taken the chance of saying it *in public.* I think a lot of Indian people were thinking, "Who the hell is this kid?" And second, they were thinking, "He's gonna make us look dumb." Looking back, I now understand what made people so nervous. There is a fine line between laughing and being laughed at, and my own people wanted to be sure that I understood that difference. I do. I always have.

With time, the Indian community came to realize that ethnic jokes could be reinvented—that we could laugh at ourselves with authority, unlike those who'd laughed out of ignorance in the past. Slowly, over time, my comedy entered the mainstream. I developed a real following, and people—red, white, brown and black—were all enjoying it. Then the Indian community relaxed a bit. My people kind of sat back and claimed me as their own. "That's our Russell," I would hear. "He's one of us." In some ways, I'm glad they were cautious, because it meant I had to earn their trust. When you're the first at anything, you're going to be the first to run into problems, and that's what happened to me when I decided to take on comedy about my own people. But no matter what, I get the badge of merit: I get to say that I was the first, and nobody can take that away from me.

CHAPTER 13

ENGLAND . . . AAAAH!!

IN JUNE 1995, I met my dear friend, the British stand-up comedian Junior Simpson. He came to Toronto on vacation with his then girlfriend, Cheryl. I met him by chance at the Nubian show at Yuk Yuk's. He was auditing the show to see if he could get a spot on it. We ended up hanging out and hitting it off. I took him around to a few clubs and got him some spots. He told me I should come to England, where he would hook me up with some work, or at least introduce me to some people who could get me some work.

So in September of '95, after taping my *Comics* episode, I went to England to see what was happening. The first show that Junior got me on was a show for a black audience in Redding. I did okay, not great, but I was just trying to figure out my footing. I did a few more shows, and once I got the hang of it over there, I kept going back to England and making pretty good loot too . . . well, at the time, it was considered pretty good loot. I'd be making two hundred pounds a show over there, whereas I'd be making two hundred dollars a show over here. There were no Indian comics there at the time, so it was fresh and new to the crowds. There's also a huge Indian population over there that was not being serviced. I was doing the mainstream circuit—clubs like Jongleurs and the Comedy Store. Things went very well because the demographics of the UK are very much like the demographics of Canada. It was just like home, but with a different accent. The other comics on those shows were guys like Keith Fields, Sean Meo, Jeff Green and Junior Simpson.

I had secured a British agent, John Keyes, and he started getting me more and more work. John was a little Jewish guy who would take any gig anywhere for any price. I remember one Saturday night in '96, I did five shows in one night at three different venues. First, I did the opening spot at the Comedy Store in London. They would have three comics on at the beginning of the night, then they'd have a break and have two more comics in the second half. Every club did that, and every comic had twenty minutes. There were no headliners. So I did the opening spot at the Comedy Store, then took the tube over to

Camden, did the closing spot of the early show, then broke out of there and did another show somewhere around Golders Green. Then I came back and did the opening spot on the late show at the Store and then the closing spot back at Camden.

I would stay with my family in South Harrow whenever I went to England—with Aunty Val and Uncle Ron, their daughter, Charlene (a.k.a. "Madwoman" or "Newman"), and their son, Darren, who was and still is the best. Darren and I are basically the same person: we have the exact same interests, except for his love of Elvis and my love of KISS. That "stani bastard" really put up with a lot. I would sleep in Darren's bed and he slept on the floor. His room was *tiny*. It was smaller than my walk-in closet now. Both of us would sleep in there, but he was the world's loudest snorer. We developed a system: I would just tap him on the shoulder and he would turn over, because he would snore only when he slept on his back. He would work from seven in the morning until three in the afternoon, come home, have a nap and then drive me to whatever gig I had. Sometimes, when it was late at night and we'd be on the M40 motorway driving back from Birmingham to London, he would be so tired that he'd fall asleep in the driver's seat and I would steer from the passenger side. He did all that driving for a good solid few years. None of my career in England would have been possible without Aunty Val and Uncle Ron, who let me stay in their house for free, fed me, did my laundry, or Darren, a guy who's more like a brother than a cousin. Between them and Junior, so much became possible. I didn't realize the connection that Junior and I had until I was best man at his wedding. When Junior gave his speech, he talked about how much I reminded him of his

My cousin Darren and me squaring off to Marquess of Queensberry rules.

late brother. I hadn't known this before his speech, and there was not a dry eye in the house after he spoke, not even my own.

I continued going back and forth to the UK for almost six or seven years, at first for a couple of weeks, then it turned into three weeks and then a month and then longer. I still played gigs back home in between the UK gigs. From England, I also ended up working in places I never in my life thought I'd perform in: Sweden, Belgium, Ireland, Amsterdam, Hong Kong, Singapore, South Africa—and let's not forget Denmark. I should point out that the Danes were the most flat-out racist of all the people I met. One guy told me to my face, "We don't like *your people* over here."

"We don't like *your people* over here."

"Canadians?" I asked him.

"No, Pakistanis."

"Oh, well, I'm Canadian."

To which he replied, "I guess that's okay then."

The one place I really loved going to was Ireland, both Northern Ireland and the Republic of Ireland. The first time I went to Northern Ireland, I did a show in Belfast. I think it was late '95 or early '96. I called my mom to tell her I was performing in Northern Ireland, and at the time my mom was working with this Northern Irish woman, Margaret McGee. So my mom says, "Oh, be careful! Don't tell them you're Catholic over there." I quickly learned it wasn't me they didn't like, it was the English. I also got the feeling that when they looked at me, they weren't thinking, "Oh look, I bet he's Catholic." Nevertheless, I was still nervous about going there. My first gig in Belfast was at the Empire, an old church that was converted into a pub. We had these tiny-ass hotel rooms at the Regency Hotel, which is right across the street. The show was hosted by Paddy Kielty, who was becoming a huge star in Ireland. He was just on fire. I had an English girl named Jo Caulfield opening for me and she got booed off. This made me nervous, but when I went up the crowd loved me and I got an encore. It wasn't that Jo was terrible—it's just that she was English.

Every time I went to Northern Ireland I'd have a great time, I'd get an encore, and then we'd do Derry the next night—Londonderry. You knew better than to call it Londonderry when you were there; you'd call it Derry, the way the locals do. I love the Irish. They were great. Cool, smart, edgy. They remind me of Canadians in that they're kind of the outsider country that's associated with the bigger country. They have an edge about them. They know what's going on and can see everything.

I played the Edinburgh Festival in Scotland in the summer of 2000 and I hated it. Not Edinburgh—the festival. The show was called "Russell Peters: Comedy Chameleon," but I wanted to call it "Russell Peters: Stand-Up Chameleon. I was playing a one-man show for five weeks, seven nights a week, at 11:45 P.M. On Mondays and Tuesdays, there would be two, maybe three, people in the audience. Playing Edinburgh was considered a big deal back then, but to me it was terrible.

Back home in Canada, my standing rose because I was in the UK all the time. I was no longer a viable option for Yuk Yuk's to book. So where a lot of Canadian comics were starting to feel trapped playing the Yuk Yuk's Canadian circuit—same bars, same cities, same shitty pay—I was over in England, getting laid and getting paid. The comics outside the Yuk Yuk's group were playing even shittier gigs. If Yuk Yuk's had taken O'Toole's on a Saturday night, the outsiders would take Dave's Bar and Grill and play for twelve people who didn't pay to see their comedy and didn't give a shit that they were standing there doing their act. But because I had played all of the shitty gigs in Canada, it really helped my stand-up in the UK.

Those crappy shows made me fearless. I was like, "What are you guys gonna do? I've played worse gigs than this." However, in the UK the audiences were spending money, treating it like a night out. They were getting drinks, having food and really taking in a show. They were all "hip hip hooray" and excited, whereas in Canada it was more like people sitting there with their arms crossed: "Go ahead. Make me laugh, fuckface." The deck was a little bit more stacked against you in Canada. On my trips back home I'd stock up on Cadbury's chocolate and Thornton's toffee for Mom and good booze for dad—Chivas Royal Salute, Johnnie Walker Black, Gold or even Green.

In the UK, Indians refer to themselves as Asians, unlike in North America, where we generally think of Asians as being Chinese, Japanese, Korean, and so on. In early 2000, I hosted an Asian stand-up special for the BBC, called *Masala Malai Mix* or something equally retardedly named. Anyway, the show was basically showcasing new South Asian comics on TV. They really liked the way I hosted it and offered me a talk show called (another dumb name) *Network East Late* on BBC Two. It was a revamp of a Saturday afternoon show called *Network East*, which they decided to turn into a late-night chat show on Thursday nights with a younger, hipper edge to it. My co-host was Laila Rouass, who was this really hot chick.

We recorded the show at the Sound Republic Bar in Leicester Square. It was a good idea, but the producers had their heads up their asses. Just because it was the Asian programming unit, they made the show everything Indian, and I was like, "Come on, man. Indian people don't do this much Indian shit in their lifetime." So all the guests were Indian . . . basically, if you were Indian and had worked as an extra somewhere, you'd be on the show.

I understand they were trying to showcase our culture, but at the same time they weren't thinking broadly enough, and it really bothered me. The first season was a little painful. My first guest was Aamir Khan, a big Bollywood star who had that movie *Lagaan* out at the time. I had never watched a Bollywood movie in my life, so I didn't know who he was. The producers gave me the movie to watch, and I remember falling asleep before the opening credits finished—it was that boring to me. (I know other people didn't find it boring, and it actually went on to set all kinds of records in India and was even nominated for an Academy Award—but hey, what do I know?)

Thing was, when I interviewed him on the show, he was really into himself. He acted like a fucking prick—and I'm not afraid to say that either. During commercial breaks, a lot of the girls would start screaming and I leaned in to him and I said, "That's gotta be pretty cool, huh?" trying to bring him back to reality, or at least relate to him as a man and not just some celebrity. He just ignored me. That was my first experience interviewing somebody, and I didn't like it.

It wasn't until the second season that I found my legs on that show, and I started to have a bit more fun with it and loosen up a little. And much like my live act, where I'm only as good as my audience, my interviewing was only as good as my guests, and let me tell you, we had some pretty uninteresting guests. You can only do so much with people with no personality.

My favourite guest was this Indian woman who did some sort of holistic medicine, like pressure points and stuff; she was a lot of fun and really funny. I don't remember her name, but she was like the holistic healer for celebrities like Liz Hurley and Princess Diana. She was pretty connected in that world. I remember she was showing me a pressure point on my leg. She said that if you kept rubbing this one part of your leg, it would stimulate your libido. And if you rubbed another part of your leg, it was good for your bowel movements—it'd loosen you up. I remember making a joke, saying, "All right, guys: if you're trying this at home, don't screw this up, because you don't want to be with your woman and rub the wrong part of your leg—you'll shit your pants instead of getting a hard-on." She was the most fun interview that I did.

We did two seasons of six episodes. I was asked to come back to host a third season, but I couldn't because I had started appearing in a Canadian sitcom, *Lord Have Mercy*. My love affair with the UK ended in 2002, when I realized that I was falling into the circuit over there, doing the same gigs over and over again. It was no different than being back home and playing Barrie, Sault Ste. Marie, Timmins, Sudbury . . .

I have really mixed feelings about England. On the one hand, it became a place where I could develop my material when no one else was interested. I was given my own talk show. I was paid more money than I could make back home. On the other hand, I just feel like the English are being ripped off by their government with their ridiculous cost of living—believe me, it is the most expensive country on the planet—and their standard of living kind of sucks. Do people really need to live in such stupid small houses? Their tiny roads and tiny cars, the weather, a class system that says you should just stay where you are . . . all of these things drive me crazy about that country, but hey, it did give me this language that I'm writing in, so thanks, England!

I ultimately returned to the UK in the summer of 2006, when CAA convinced Live Nation UK to book me into the Shaw Theatre. It was a small theatre of about four hundred seats on Euston Road. It was my first solo theatre show in London and my first time back in several years. I ended up selling out the two shows in less than forty-eight hours. I was actually kind of pissed, because I knew I could have played a larger venue, but the promoter wasn't convinced of my ability to sell tickets. Fact is, we were kind of lucky to have Live Nation

UK come on board with me at that time. All the other promoters had turned CAA down. Later that year, I came back and played the Hammersmith Apollo, which has about 3,800 seats. The show sold out very quickly and opened up standing room only. There were people along the back walls and spilling into the aisles. It was great. I returned to the Hammersmith for two shows in 2007, and they also sold out crazy fast.

When we put the tickets on sale, we sold nine thousand on the first day.

In 2009, I returned to London with my Twentieth-Anniversary Tour and played the O2 Arena. When we put the tickets on sale, we sold nine thousand on the first day, which I never expected. I ended up setting a new UK attendance record for a one-off comedy show, almost sixteen thousand people—and my biggest show worldwide. The previous record holder was Chris Rock. I never expected those kinds of numbers. I wasn't thrilled with my performance that night because I was just in the early stages of writing the act that I'm doing today. I was supposed to be doing my "greatest hits" of the past twenty years, but when I got on stage, I couldn't bring myself to do it—because comedy is all about the surprise of the punch line.

Have you ever had someone tell you the same joke twice? It's not that great the second time. That's where musicians get a pass. They can write one or two great songs and just keep playing them over and over. A comedian may write ten great bits but can't just keep repeating them. They can be brought out again eventually, but not until many, many years later.

I thought I could have done a better show and felt badly that, in my opinion, I had let the fans down that night. Funny thing is, I got more positive feedback from the fans after that show than I have for any other.

People in the UK got me early. They understood me and were early supporters of what I was doing. Those audiences, from the Comedy Store, to Jongleurs, to all the pubs from Newcastle to Dover, allowed me to get better and become more confident. I thank them for that.

I thought it was fitting that I close this chapter with an email excerpt from a promoter who turned me down for a show in London in 2006:

" . . . While I think that Russell is obviously a top class club comedian I didn't feel that his material is distinctive enough for it to break through over here. Personally, I thought that I had seen similar material done better before . . . my opinion is that Russell will find it hard to break into this market with his existing material. Moreover, I think that it would be a mistake to rely on the UK Asian audience which is not guaranteed . . . I'm sorry, but I don't think I can get behind this one . . ."

This man was a visionary.

CHAPTER 14

SOUTH AFRICA

I ABSOLUTELY looooove South Africa. It's beautiful and fascinating. The different cultures and people and the dynamics between all of them: black, white, cape coloured, Indian, Zulu and Xhosa. On my first visit to South Africa in October 2001, it was all new and amazing to me. This was a country that my father had told me about as a kid, and one I never ever thought I'd get to visit.

When I finally got there to play the Cape Town Comedy Festival, it was the beginning of an adventure that would keep me coming back for more. Never in my life had I seen so many beautiful women who were so out of my league. No offence to suicide bombers, but South Africa is paradise.

I was thirty-one years old and had never had a drink in my life. After one of the shows, some of the other comics and I went out to a casino, where we met this really hot coloured girl. She started hanging out with us, having some drinks. I asked her, "What are you drinking?"

"Blah, blah, blah, why don't you have some?" is what I remember her saying.

"Umm, I don't drink," I confessed.

But she was so hot that I said, "Okay," and tried her fruity little cocktail. It was actually really good. I couldn't taste any alcohol in it at all.

"So, do you drink a lot?" I asked her.

To which she gave me the best reply in the world: "I do, because it makes me horny . . . and I hate to be horny alone . . ."

Let's have another one! She had another, and another, and so did I. After a while, our entire group headed off to a cigar lounge. We sat down in these really nice armchairs and I was feeling good; I was starting to get a nice buzz going, I had on a great suit and Hot Coloured Girl was looking good-to-go. I was feeling pimp, so I ordered a cigar. Now, even though I didn't drink, I did know that you were supposed to drink Cognac when you have a cigar. Thing is, I wasn't sure how to drink Cognac. I asked the girl. She said, "You just shoot it." So I did, and it burned all the way down.

One of the reasons I'd never drunk before was because I didn't like the way alcohol tasted and smelled. I was also a bit nervous about what kind of drunk I'd be. My dad and some of my uncles could get a bit argumentative and aggressive when they had one too many; turned out that I just felt happy. Not angry or aggressive, just good and giggly. I even felt fine the next day.

I started crying about my dad and the news that I'd got that day.

The rest of the night was great. A few more fruity cocktails, and Hot Coloured Girl and I ended up back at my hotel . . .

It would be three years before I got drunk again. In February 2004, the day the doctor told my brother and me that Dad had only six months to live. That night I went out with a group of friends to a club on Adelaide Street and I drank a lot of vodka—too much vodka. I ended up projectile vomiting. I remember my cousin Bob taking me outside and walking me around the block to sober up, and I started crying about my dad and the news that I'd got that day. The doctor was wrong, however, or maybe he was just being kind, but the six months actually turned out to be just one month.

I returned to South Africa in June 2002, and this time I was hosting a show at the Durban Comedy Festival. I was there for two weeks, and even though it was my first time in Durban, for some reason I felt like I was at home and was completely at ease. Maybe it's because Durban has the highest population of Indians outside of India and I grew up in Brampton, which feels much the same way. Anyway, I loved Durban. Still do. The shows were great and the people received me as if they'd known me all my life. They treated me like gold. I stayed at this Holiday Inn right on the ocean, and from my room I could see sharks, whales and dolphins off in the distance.

Toyota was a sponsor of those first shows in Durban, and they told me they'd give me a car to drive. Toyota had set up this brand new Corolla Sport on display in front of the theatre where I was performing, so I figured they'd give me something like that to drive around in.

The next day they showed up at my hotel with this old-ass, fucked-up 1994 Corolla with manual windows and no stereo. I'm not sure what they were thinking. That night, I went on stage and made fun of Toyota for giving me such a shit car. The next day, they pulled their sponsorship and took back the piece-of-shit car they'd given me to drive.

I liked Durban so much that I actually considered buying a house there. You can get a wicked mansion for just over two hundred grand. But it's a long commute back and forth between L.A. or Toronto.

I was treated like a superstar and once again had an awesome time. Crazy things happened.

In November and December of 2002, I once again returned to South Africa, and it was insanity. I was treated like a superstar and once again had an awesome time. Crazy things happened. One of the morning radio shows did this thing where they asked if any of their listeners had slept with a celebrity. A girl phoned in and said that she had. When they asked who, she said my name. The papers ran a piece about me being seen with some girl at Umhlanga Rocks (a seaside resort near Durban).

On that trip there was this Indian guy who owned a cell phone company, and he gave me his Smart car to drive. To me, the Smart car looked like a giant nose, and I have a giant nose. So it was like a giant nose driving a giant nose. The Smart car was fine, but there was this one particularly windy day when it felt like the car was going to be blown over, which made me nervous as hell. BMW was a sponsor of these shows. The BMW guy came saw me driving the Smart car and asked, "What the hell are you driving?" He got me a 330i convertible and then a 745il. The other car that he let me drive was his X5 SUV. I would get bored after the shows, so I would go for late-night drives.

One night, I was driving around Umhlanga Rocks, looking at houses. The X5 had GPS on it, which was still new at that time. As I was driving,

I saw this dirt road. I thought, *Hey, I'm in an all-wheel-drive SUV. There's a dirt road. I've got GPS and I'm in Africa; let's see where this road goes.* There was a sign for a nursery along this dirt road, so I figured I'd drive up to the nursery and turn around. Unfortunately, the nursery was right there, as soon as you turned the corner. I looked ahead and saw that the road continued, as the GPS confirmed. Hmmm . . . I'm in Africa. Maybe I'll see a lion or something! As I drove, I glanced at the GPS and could see all this blue near me, so I figured, *Oh neat, maybe this road will take me to a secret beach or something.* Not sure what I thought I'd do once I got to the "secret beach," but hey. The road started curving, running parallel to the ocean, with a highway between myself and the water.

As I drove in the pitch darkness, I now realized that the dirt road was just a single lane. I could only go forward, but I was also thinking that I'd catch the highway at some point and be able to get off. I drove under an overpass, with the highway above me. Okay, this should be it. Suddenly I went up an incline and the dirt road had turned into two cement tracks. I was on a bridge of some kind. Fuck! I couldn't back up, because I was afraid I'd fall off the road, so I kept going forward. The

I looked around and saw that I was now driving through a squatters' camp, which looked exactly like they do in those UNICEF commercials.

bridge ended and the road became really wonky and fucked-up with potholes and ditches. I looked around and saw that I was now driving through a squatters' camp, which looked exactly like they do in those UNICEF commercials. It was now past midnight, there was nobody outside and it was dead quiet. From out of nowhere, this dog started barking and scared the shit out of me. The GPS said that the road ended just ahead, and I started freaking out. I decided that now was the time to turn around. After a quick three-point turn, I looked at the GPS and the screen had turned blank. No roads, no ocean, no highway, no nuthin'! So I made a call to one of my cab-driver buddies down by the beach. Sammy, one of the drivers I had befriended, answered.

"Yo! I'm kind of lost."

"Where are you?"

"Oh my God! What are you doing there? Get out of there now! A cop was shot there just two weeks ago!"

"I went for a drive at Umhlanga Rocks and turned on that dirt road past the nursery. I'm in the squatters' camp . . ."

"Oh my God! What are you doing there? Get out of there now! A cop was shot there just two weeks ago!"

The irony was that this camp was less than a mile away from the richest part of Durban.

Sammy stayed on the phone with me and guided me out of the camp. He and the other drivers stayed on the line until I was safely back on the main road. He told me to come meet him downtown. The drivers were all waiting for me when I got there. They said that I should probably keep a gun with me if I was going to be driving around like that, and Sammy offered me one of his pistols for the duration of my stay. I told them that I would be fine.

These drivers were all Indian guys. They were decent, good guys. They all carried guns with them—not to be bad-asses or anything, but just because they felt that they needed them for their own safety. I got to know them through one of the Indian street kids who stayed near my hotel. I made friends with this kid, whose name I can't remember now. He was a good kid, but was pretty much homeless. A lot of the kids just hung out on the beach and sniffed glue all day. He introduced me to the cab drivers and they all thought I was all right for being cool with the kid.

In 2003, I came back to South Africa again. The movie I was supposed to be working on had been cancelled and SA offered me a chance to make some money. I was so desperate for cash at that time that I accepted this awful deal for $700 U.S. per day. Now, I know that may not sound too bad, but here's the thing: I was there for maybe five or six weeks, and the tour was completely sold out. The promoter (that fucker) had tons of sponsors and they just kept adding shows, sometimes two a night without a bump in pay. Seven hundred dollars was less than maybe five per cent of what they were actually making. They made a shitload off of me and I never forgot it.

During that trip I called Sammy, and it turned out that he was now getting married. He invited me and the other comics on the show—Jean Paul, Paul Chowdhry and Rasool Somji—to come to his wedding. We got to the reception and he was very happy to see me. He saw me and said, "I want you to hold the wedding rings, the money and, here, hold my gun too!"

"What do you mean?" I asked him.

"I don't trust anybody here. I trust you."

He took off his wedding band and his wife's rings and gave them to me to hold. I put the envelopes of cash inside and the rings in my jacket pocket and put the gun in my waistband in the small of my back.

After the reception was over, Sammy met me in the parking lot and all the other drivers were there. I handed the rings and money over to him as well as the handgun. One of the other drivers saw me with the gun. "Hey, you've got a pistol? Do you want to hold mine too?" he yelled across, smiling through his gold teeth.

One day, I was walking outside my hotel and this guy came up to me like he knew me. "Uncle! Uncle!" I didn't recognize him, but it was the kid I'd befriended the year before. Not being all that kid oriented, I failed to realize that kids grow. I invited him and his mom to the hotel for dinner that night. Afterwards, I took them shopping for new shoes and a bunch of other stuff they needed.

Over the course of these first few trips to South Africa, I must have slept with anywhere from a dozen to two dozen different women. I even had a hat trick, three different women within twenty-four hours. It was pretty wild. From the guns to the girls, to the squatters' camps, to the mansions, to the great people that I met, South Africa had it all.

My only regret was that I never had the money to take my dad there. He would have loved it too—Dad had always dreamed of one day going to one of the game reserves and sleeping under the stars surrounded by the lions that I'd gone in search of on that dirt road.

PART FIVE

FULL

CIRCLE

RACIALLY, I'M AN INDIAN MAN. BUT THERE ARE THINGS THAT HAPPEN CULTURALLY THAT YOU WILL FIND UNACCEPTABLE IF YOU WERE NOT RAISED IN THAT PART OF THE WORLD.

Like the fact that in India, grown-ass men—GROWN-ASS MEN—hold hands with other men and walk down the street like everything's okay. And they don't just hold hands. They're holding pinkies! To them, there's nothing gay about it—"I'm holding my friend's hand. What's gay about that?"—but over here, there is no acceptable time for two straight men to ever touch hands. Ever.

Have you ever walked to the mall with one of your guy friends and your hand accidentally bumps into his and you say, "WHAT-THE-FUCK-IS-WRONG-WITH-YOU? Get *off* me!" But in India, grown-ass men hold hands, and the best thing about it is that these guys still mac on chicks. Some of these guys act like thugs. They'll be holding pinkies and eyeballing you, like they're trying to start some shit.

I was at a beach in Bombay hanging out, and this gang of seventeen—no, sixteen, because seventeen's an odd number and that would leave some guy alone not holding hands. . . . Anyhow, this gang is walking across the beach, holding pinkies, and giving everybody dirty looks . . . while wearing dress pants and flip-flops. And so I asked myself, *How do you start a fight while holding another man's hand?*

CHAPTER 15

VERNON FORREST R.I.P.

I LOVE boxing. And like my dad, I've admired boxers since I was a kid. Over the years, I've been lucky enough to meet many of my boxing heroes and actually become friends with a few of them. But none of them had the impact on me that Vernon Forrest did.

I met Vernon in Atlanta on my birthday in 2007, when I was headlining a weekend at the Punchline Comedy Club. My opener that weekend was a comic named King Kedar, and he was friends with Vernon. King knew that I was a boxing nut, and I asked him to invite Vernon to one of my shows.

That's right: porn. I don't deny being well versed in the subject, and so was Vernon.

Vernon came to my Saturday night show and then we hung out backstage afterwards. He was a former WBC welterweight and two-time WBC super welterweight champion who had defeated Shane Mosley twice in 2002. He was also a U.S. Olympian in 1992. Based on his accomplishments, he could have been a complete dick, but he wasn't. He was this gentle, soft-spoken guy who liked to laugh, and we really hit it off. We talked a lot about boxing, but where we really connected was on the subject of porn, of all things. That's right: porn. I don't deny being well versed in the subject, and so was Vernon. I told Vernon that I'd hook him up at the AVN (*Adult Video News*) Awards in Vegas.

My friend Yoshi arranged the tickets to the AVNs in January for Vernon, and my girlfriend at the time, actress Sunny Leone, who was also at the awards, made sure that Vernon was taken care of. After the awards, Vernon came down to L.A. and stayed with me for a couple of weeks and we really bonded. We both had non-traditional jobs that gave us a lot of freedom when we weren't on the road, or in his case, training. Vernon was easy-going and not high-maintenance at all. He didn't ask for anything and didn't expect anything. He'd come up poor and now had a lot of people around him, clinging onto him and expecting shit from him. I didn't expect anything. We both had money, but I would never let him pay for anything. That was something that was completely new to him. He was just so used to picking up the tab whenever he was with his crew. Though he was a five-time world champion, he would never fly himself first class or put himself up in the best hotels. He was practical and realistic. Whenever we were together we'd just hang out and talk shit. I can still hear him now, as we'd walk through the Beverly Center and he'd see some hot chick: "Hey shorty! Holla holla holla!" That shit just made me laugh.

I can still hear him now, as we'd walk through the Beverly Center and he'd see some hot chick: "Hey shorty! Holla holla holla!"

On July 24, 2009, I performed the largest indoor comedy show in Just for Laughs history. The show was at the Bell Centre in Montreal and wrapped the summer leg of my Twentieth-Anniversary Tour. It was great and we had a great time at the afterparty, where Spin, Scratch and I all took turns DJing. Just for Laughs even presented me with an award in recognition of the show.

After the party, I decided to drive home. I was sick of staying in hotels and just wanted to sleep in my own bed in Toronto. I also had a new girlfriend at the time and wanted to see her, too. When I got home, I slept all day Saturday and was still tired, so I went to bed early that night (well, early for me, which would have been around 2 A.M. or so).

On Sunday I got up early and saw a missed call on my phone from Vernon's assistant, Armica. She had called at three-thirty in the morning, which was strange. Without even checking the message, I called her back. She started crying and then said that Vernon had been murdered that night, a victim of a carjacking. I don't remember what I said, but I know I just started bawling like a little baby. My girlfriend had a wedding to go to, so I dropped her home—she was still new at the time, so I did my best to keep it together in front of her.

When I got back home, I really started freaking out. I was crying uncontrollably. My head felt like a tornado. I paced around the house with my heart racing. I thought I was going crazy. I sat in my Jacuzzi. I sat in my sauna. I put on the Iron Maiden DVD *Flight 666* and played it full blast. As the day progressed, I started texting my girlfriend, "Where are you? Why aren't you here taking care of me?" She simply replied that she was at her friend's wedding and that there was nothing she could do. She was not comforting or understanding at all.

That day, the story of Vernon's murder was on the news and I was getting more details from mutual friends in Atlanta. The night he was killed, he was training at a local gym in Atlanta. He had his eleven-year-old godson with him. At around 11 P.M., after training, he'd stopped at a gas station to put air in one of his tires when a guy came up to him and asked for money. Vernon took out his wallet and the guy snatched it and started running. Vernon reached into his car, grabbed his gun and took off after the guy. He chased him around a corner and shots were exchanged. Vernon was shot seven or eight times with a semi-automatic pistol in the torso, legs and head. His godson had gone into the gas station to get help and wasn't injured.

The day I got the news about Vernon, I had tickets to see Richard Cheese's very funny lounge act at the Phoenix in Toronto. I was really looking forward to the show, but that night I wasn't in any mood for comedy and just wanted to go home. I hadn't felt that fucked up since my dad died.

A week later, my brother and I flew down to Atlanta for Vernon's funeral. It was a massive event at this huge Baptist church. A lot of boxers were there, including Evander Holyfield. The service was very elaborate, and I was listed as a pallbearer on the memorial booklet. One of Vernon's friends, Les King, had gone up to the altar to say a few words and I went up with him. I thought that I might say

Ultimately, that's what I was mourning: all the stuff that we'd never get to do together.

something, too, but as I stood there I knew that I wouldn't be able to keep it together, so I just stood alongside Les silently and then sat back down. I don't know if it was the kind of send-off that Vernon would have wanted, given how low-key he was.

I was glad that I went to the funeral. Although I didn't want to say goodbye to my friend, I knew that I had to and that I'd feel strange if I hadn't gone. They say that when we mourn someone, we're not grieving for them, we're grieving for ourselves. My friendship with Vernon was still new and still growing. We had plans for the future. Ultimately, that's what I was mourning: all the stuff that we'd never get to do together.

CHAPTER 16

MOTHERLAND

THE FIRST time I went to India was in 1976, when I was six years old. The whole family spent Christmas in Calcutta with my grandmother, KK, Uncle Maurice, Uncle Roger and his wife at the flat on Elliot Road. My grandmother gave me a cowboy outfit as a Christmas present. It came with a vest, a cowboy hat, a holster and a gun.

In 1982, we returned to India again. My brother and I stayed with our dad in Burhanpur while Mom went ahead to Calcutta to see her family. While we were in Burhanpur, Dad taught both of us how to use an air rifle to shoot birds and for target practice. He'd take us for long walks into the surrounding hills where he spent his childhood. The hills weren't as lush as they were when he was younger—most of the trees had been cut down for firewood by the villagers. The servants would come with us. These were the same guys who'd been working for Dad's family for the past thirty-plus years.

With the deforestation and dwindling amount of big game in the area, these treks into the hills were more about nostalgia than anything else. The chances of actually seeing a tiger, leopard or cheetah were pretty slight. However, at one point Dad pointed to a paw print in a muddy gulley. "You see that?" he said. "A tiger was just here."

Returning to the house from one of these walks, we were crossing a field. As we walked, I heard a hissing sound—*ssssssssss*. Nobody else heard it but me.

"Dad! Stop! Stop moving," I said.

"What? What is it?"

"Listen."

Everyone froze, and then they heard it too. We all looked down, and right by one of the servants' feet was an asp, poised to bite. My dad immediately moved to get his gun into position, but I had the air rifle ready and just pointed it downward. "Pop?" My dad nodded and I squeezed off a shot. Somehow, I managed to hit the snake right in the head and kill it on the spot.

The servants were not only relieved but impressed and treated me like a champ. I didn't know what they were saying in Urdu, but I know they wanted to carry me home on their shoulders. Dad was impressed, too, which was not a minor accomplishment. I don't know if the servant realized just how close he came to being shot in the ankle or the foot. It was a lucky shot, and I knew it.

I loved that in Burhanpur I could be outdoors and run around and explore the compound. But as I'd be leaving the house, my dad would warn me, "Watch out for cobras . . . and don't fall in the well!"

At the house in Burhanpur there was no running water, but there was electricity, which would usually go out in the evenings because of rolling power cuts. Sometimes we'd eat dinner by gaslight and Dad, our grandmother and her brother, Uncle Jumbo, would tell us stories about our grandfather and reminisce about "the old days" when everyone was still alive and the family—my uncles, aunts, cousins and friends from the city who would come and stay with them—would all be together at the house.

The best analogy I can make to the house in Burhanpur is the family cottage where everybody stayed every summer. There was a massive tiger skin mounted on the main wall of the dining room, which was the focal point of the house, smack dab in the centre when you walked in from the enclosed verandah. All the bedrooms opened onto it, and the kitchen was at the back. According to my dad, when the house was full there'd be cots in the dining room and all over the house where everyone would sleep. My brother and I shared a bed on one side of the house, where we'd sleep under a mosquito net at night. The toilet was essentially a wooden chair with a hole cut in the bottom, beneath which there'd be an aluminum bucket with a handle. A little aluminum lid sat on top of the hole.

As I said before, Dad grew up hunting, fishing and camping in the hills around the house. All of the men in the family were known as *shikars* (hunters) by the local villagers and were often called upon to rid villages of nuisance tigers and other predators. These were usually old animals that couldn't hunt very well anymore, so they'd wander into villages looking for easier kills—farm animals and humans. As Dad liked to say, "Man is the easiest thing for it to kill." Dad shot five man-eating tigers over his life, and even though these were problem animals and the kills were sanctioned by the local authorities, he came to regret them later as tigers became an endangered species. He felt a lot of guilt about it. But at the time, it was the villagers who were endangered, not the tigers.

The villagers looking on after a man-eater was killed.

Dad loved to tell us about the last tiger that he shot. He kept the skin, with the taxidermied head still attached, its mouth open in a roar, and brought it to Canada with him. From the tip of the tail to the tip of the nose, the skin measures almost twelve feet and is eight feet across. When people came to our house to visit, he'd pull out the tiger skin, spread it across the living room and tell the guests about his last encounter with a man-eater . . .

A villager was working in the fields near a local village. He was cutting long grass with a scythe and didn't see the old tiger sleeping nearby. The tip of his scythe accidentally glanced the sleeping tiger and startled it. Instinctively, the tiger reached up and swatted the villager, knocking his head into his chest cavity. The slightly embellished version of the story goes that the villagers spent a week looking for the guy's head, only to find it in his ribcage. Given Dad's reputation, the villagers came to him and asked him to hunt down the decapitating tiger.

Dad with the last tiger he shot.

Dad took one of my grandmother's best goats and tied it to a tree in the jungle where this tiger was said to roam. He set himself up in a *machan*—a kind of hunting blind you make in a tree so that you can watch for prey from above—and waited for nightfall. After a few hours, the goat suddenly started to get antsy, pacing and bleating loudly. Dad knew that this meant the tiger was close, and he started to get his rifle ready for the shot. There was a full moon that night, and Dad could see the tiger in the clearing, not far from his tree.

The startled tiger looked up and immediately launched himself into the air, straight for Dad.

It was low to the ground and ready to pounce on the goat, but Dad realized he didn't have a clear shot. He grabbed his flashlight and tapped it against the barrel of the rifle. The startled tiger looked up and immediately launched himself into the air, straight for Dad. His rifle ready, Dad squeezed off a single shot that hit the tiger square in the chest, instantly killing it and knocking it to the ground. He waited in the *machan* for a while, then threw a few stones at the tiger to make sure it was dead before he came down from the tree. His mother was very happy that the goat came back home in one piece.

Dad remained fascinated by tigers, and all wildlife, for the rest of his life. He made regular donations to the World Wildlife Fund, the SPCA and the Humane Society.

I have to admit that, on all those trips to India, the dirt and poverty never registered with me. I don't know why. It almost seemed like, "Okay, so this is how people live in India. It's just a bit different than Canada." I played with the servants' kids who were my age. I didn't speak Hindi or Urdu and they didn't speak English. We just kind of ran around the compound—whether at the house in Burhanpur or in the front compound of my grandmother's apartment in Calcutta. There were also a few Anglo-Indian kids living in the buildings, so I'd play with them too.

I returned to India in 1998 with my mom. I really wanted to go back and was excited to be there. We stayed with Uncle Maurice in Calcutta (my grandmother and KK had long passed, but Uncle Maurice, Aunty Jennifer and my cousins Steven and Tanya still lived in the same flat). Mom and I shared a bed in the back room—yes, that's right: at the age of twenty-seven, I shared a bed with my mom. Once again, it goes back to my childhood view of India. The bed had a makeshift mattress, hand-stuffed with coconut hair or straw or something. After my first night on the coconut mattress, I woke up with bruises on my hips, but there was no point complaining. We couldn't afford a hotel, and I liked that we were staying in the same flat that I'd stayed in when I was six years old.

I was filled with nostalgia on that trip—memories of running around the apartment, everyone twenty years younger, my grandparents and the sense of family. The trip made me realize how much I loved India. I loved the people, the food, the culture. And the energy was incredible. In cities like Calcutta, every night seemed like Saturday night. When we were there, people would come over and visit during the week and we'd go out all the time. My uncle's flat hadn't changed in the sixteen years since my last visit. There was still no running hot water or bathtub or shower—just a concrete floor with a drain in the middle of it. The family keeps a large, red plastic garbage can in the bathroom, and when you wanted to take a shower, they'd scoop out a pot full of water, boil it on the little gas stovetop in the kitchen and then add it to the water in the garbage can and mix cold and hot together. Next, you'd scoop out a mug of lukewarm water and throw it on yourself to get wet, then soap yourself and repeat, splashing yourself until the soap was gone. It may sound like a lot of work, but hey, it's India and that's just how it is. The lifestyle of the Anglo-Indians in India isn't great. While there's a lot of wealth and a growing middle class, AIs still pretty much live below a middle-class standard. After the Brits left in 1947, we were at loose ends—and the "Indians" reclaimed their country, leaving the Anglo-Indians behind.

Growing up, I always identified myself as an Indian. People would ask me what I was, and my answer was always "Indian!" I don't think I'm different from any other first-generation kid identifying myself by where my parents came from. I was born and raised in Canada. The only Indian things about me are my parents and my skin tone. Even my name isn't "Indian." Culturally, I'm not Indian at all, and that trip to India in 1998 brought that realization home: I'm Canadian.

With that in mind, I returned to India in 2007 for my first comedy tour. I wasn't really sure exactly how my act would go over with the fans there. Let's face it: a lot of my punchlines up to then had something to do with the Indian accent, and here I was, going to the place where pretty much everyone had that accent. Would they get it? Would they get the jokes about the Chinese and all the other stuff? I had no idea, and I was a bit nervous before I did my first show in Bangalore. I chose comedian Rusty Dooley to open for me on that tour. Rusty's set consisted of a lot of impersonations from the movies and used props and music. He was completely different from any other opener that I had ever worked with, but I thought he'd be the right guy for India. Rusty had never been outside the U.S. before and was more than a bit uneasy about going to India. I remember him telling me how his mom had begged him not to go. She was afraid he'd catch AIDS and, as she told him, "Nothing's worth catching the AIDS."

When we got to India, he hardly ate anything. At breakfast, he'd just eat the chocolate off the top of the doughnuts. He was terrified of catching some disease. My security guys, Ray Ray and Shake, decided they were going to fuck with him and told him that when he was walking around town, he should walk on the balls of his feet—because, if his heels touched the ground, he'd catch a flesh-eating disease. He actually did that for about a day until my guys copped to it.

The shows were all sold out before I got there, and extra shows were being added after I landed—we even did a matinee in Delhi. The first show in Bangalore went great. The audience was smart, sharp and with me on every word and reference. I could relax now. I didn't have to worry about my act or even change anything. I just did my thing, and the tour went off well.

In Bombay, there were a few Bollywood stars at the shows. I decided to go off on them and made fun of the movies and their acting, and they loved it. I also stayed at the Taj Hotel on that trip, the exact same one that was attacked by terrorists on November 26, 2008. It was very surreal to watch the building burn on CNN. During those same attacks, the terrorists hit the Oberoi Hotel in Bombay. I had been at the Oberoi exactly one month earlier, shopping at the Gucci and Salvatore Ferragamo stores. Now, that really freaked me out. It was only a matter of four weeks from my visit to the day the Oberoi was attacked.

Despite my "Canadian-ness," I still feel at home in India. I feel comfortable and connected to my past and to my parents and grandparents.

CHAPTER 17

ROYALLY PUNK'D

IN DECEMBER 2009, I was headlining the Amman Stand-Up Comedy Festival in Amman, Jordan. Now, I know that when you think comedy, you think, "Hey, Amman, Jordan!"—which is exactly why the city puts on the festival. It wants to change the way people see Arabs and the Middle East in general, and I thought it would be pretty cool to support that.

I'd been told that the king, His Majesty King Abdullah II, was a fan of mine—he'd seen my clips on YouTube. Go figure. The first year I did the fest, he couldn't make it to my show and called me personally to apologize for not coming. He sent me a beautiful white-gold Jaeger-LeCoultre watch as a thank-you gift for doing the show. Needless to say, I knew I'd be coming back to the festival.

Once again, the king was unable to attend my shows in 2009. This time, he couldn't make it because he'd dissolved Parliament that day and was busy—okay, fine! However, he did have us—me, my brother, and comedian Gabriel Iglesias—over to the palace for a formal reception the morning of the show. That in itself was pretty cool, and so was the king. I gave him a set of *Star Trek* cuff links as a small gift. I said, "I hear you're a Trekkie."

"I *used* to be a Trekkie," he answered. I think he stopped once he became king.

This man wasn't at all what I was expecting. He is low key, charming and has a good sense of humour. He went to school in the States and the UK, so he has sort of an American/English accent. We chatted for a while in his formal reception room and he told us how sorry he was that he couldn't come to the show but asked if we'd like to come back to the palace afterwards for dinner. We all looked at each other and said, "Sure!" Once we left, we pretty much figured it wouldn't happen. I mean, he's the king, and we're a bunch of comics who got into comedy so that we wouldn't have to get real jobs! We thought he was just being polite and that "king stuff" would come up and that would be that. It was nice just to have been invited and to have met the guy.

Late that afternoon, we got word that we would actually be going to the palace after the show. My good friend, comedian Angelo Tsarouchas, was performing at the festival as well, and when my brother told him he'd be meeting the king later that night, Angelo said, "You know who I'd really like to meet? Pamela Anderson."

"What are you talking about?" my brother asked him.

"Yeah. Pamela Anderson is who I'd like to meet." Ang didn't believe that we were going to the palace after the show and was pretty stunned when we pulled up in front of it.

At some point while we were talking, I decided to tell the king he had really nice eyes. I don't know why.

We arrived at the palace at around eleven-thirty, and King Abdullah and Queen Rania met us at the door. My sister-in-law, Emma, was with us and she didn't realize it was the king and queen greeting us until we got to their family room. She was so stunned that she didn't even speak for the first fifteen minutes. Queen Rania had just returned from Paris, where she had given a speech that day. The king's brother and a few of his friends were there as well. Everyone was very nice and relaxed. The king was behind the grill and actually made us Kobe steaks and chicken for dinner!

At some point while we were talking, I decided to tell the king he had really nice eyes. I don't know why. Gabriel was like, "What, are you hitting on him or something?" I wasn't, but I happened to notice his blue eyes and couldn't help saying so. Awkward . . .

Then the king asked me what time my flight was leaving the next morning. I said, "Ten-thirty. I'm leaving the hotel at seven-thirty."

"No. That's too early. I'll call the airport. You'll leave the hotel at nine."

That's when I realized: *He's the king. He can do what he wants!* We were having a great time hanging out with him and his friends. Everyone was really nice and down to earth. We talked about politics.

The queen is really passionate about her charities and all of the problems in the region. We also talked about movies and life in L.A. The king asked what Toronto was like, since he'd never been. It was getting late, almost 3 A.M., and we didn't want to overstay our welcome. The get-together wasn't showing signs of slowing down, but my brother and I wanted to be polite and excuse ourselves at a reasonable time.

The next morning, all of us got to the airport at nine-thirty for our ten-thirty flight. There were these guys on the curb waiting for us; they took our passports and our luggage and sent us up to a VIP room. We were all chilling in this VIP room, still totally in awe that we'd had dinner with the king the night before.

At about ten to ten, an angry Arab dude walked into the room holding a passport and saying, in his angry voice, "Russell Beters!" (There's no *p* sound in Arabic, so *p*'s become *b*'s.)

I said, "That's me."

"Come with me," the Arab dude said.

I said, "No . . ." I was feeling cocky as hell at the time because I'd spent the previous night hanging out with the king.

Arab Dude said again: "Come. With. Me."

So I said, "Okay. You don't have to get all uppity."

Then he asked, "Where's your bag?"

I said, "Right here."

He said, "You have two phones." And I'm thinking, *How does this guy know how many phones I have?*

Next thing I know, he'd snatched one of my phones right out of my hand. I looked around the room at everyone, and clearly none of us knew what the hell was happening. He told me to go with him, so we left the room. Once outside, he asked me, "Do you speak Arabic?"

I said, "No."

"Huh."

Then he led me down these stairs, and I remember thinking, *Here's where I should trip him down the stairs, choke him and then run away.* But I didn't do that—where was I going to run? We got to the bottom of the stairs, and I could see these two military guys in full gear—helmets, vests, elbow pads, gloves—standing there with machine guns, pointing them right at me. At this point, my ego kicked in, and I thought, *Oh . . . Now I get it. The king must have come to the airport to say goodbye. Cool!* So I said to the guys with the machine guns, "Hey guys, don't worry. It's just me. I know the king." But these dudes were totally serious and staring me down with their guns ready to go.

Then Arab Dude led me down a hall and sat me in a room. The military guys were right behind me and followed me in. One stood behind me with his gun pointed at my head. The other stood in the doorway, pointing his weapon down the hallway. Now I was thinking, *What the hell is going on?* I looked beside me and saw a camcorder with a blanket over it. At that point, I figured out I was in an interrogation room. But just then, my Indian side kicked in, and instead of worrying about the guys with the guns, I remember thinking, *Hmm . . . that's a really old camcorder. They really need to get some new product in here.*

Then Arab Dude started to interrogate me. "Where were you last night?"

"Well, I did a show."

"And then where did you go?"

"Then I went to the palace."

"What palace?"

"What do you mean, 'What palace?!' The *king's* palace."

"Which king?"

I'm like, "The one behind you," and I pointed to the portrait of the king right behind him. There are portraits of the king and his father, King Abdullah I, everywhere in Jordan.

"Oh, you mean *my* king."

"Yeah, your king."

"Why you went?"

"Because he invited me."

"Huh," he said. Then he lit up a cigarette, and every time he wasn't looking, I was peering into the lens of the camcorder and making faces. I honestly thought the homeboy with the gun was going to shoot me in the back of the head, and if I was about to die, I at least wanted my last video to be funny.

So at this point, I started sweating—right underneath my man boobs. I was getting nervous, and it was really silent. Then all of a sudden, from the hallway, I heard a whole bunch of Arabic being yelled back and forth, and then the Arab dude interrogating me started yelling back in Arabic, and I was like, "*ARGGHH!!* What's happening?" The guy who had the machine gun pointed at me now pointed it towards the door, and then I heard, "Don't point the gun at me, fool!"

It was Gabriel Iglesias. He came into the room with a phone and passed it to me, all nervous, and I picked it up and said, "Hello? Who's this?"

That's when I heard King Abdullah's voice, saying, "Never be the first to leave a party again. You just got punk'd, Beeatch."

Even more unexpected and then having dinner with him and Her Majesty was finding out that he's a practical joker and a regular guy. I never saw it coming.

Me and King Abdullah, at 2:30 A.M., in the palace.

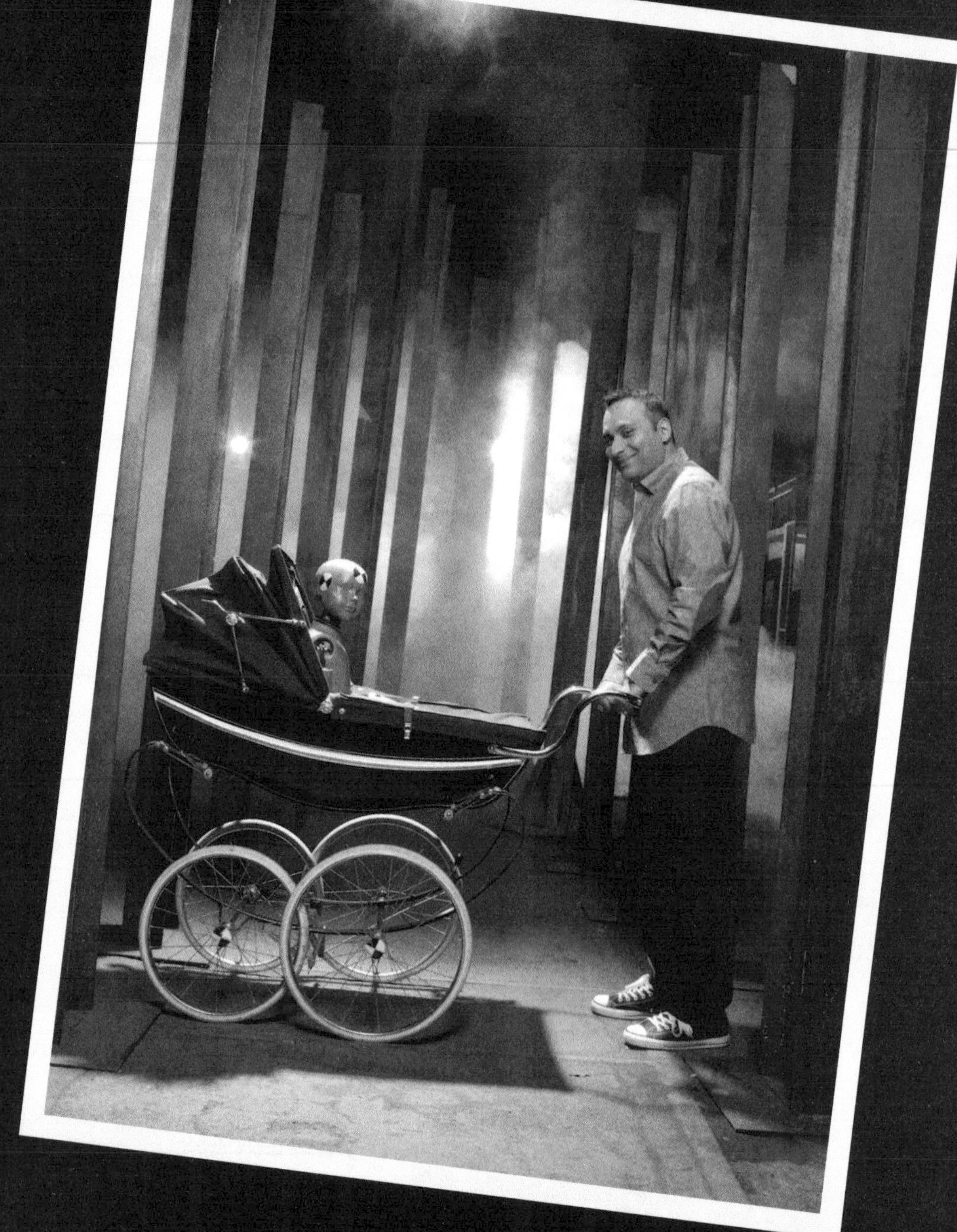

CHAPTER 18

NEXT?

IN 2010, I decided two things: I wanted to have a baby and I wanted to get married. Something inside me told me that this was the right time for both of these things to happen. Everyone around me—all of my friends, my family, even casual acquaintances—told me that I was nuts. "A baby, sure! But marriage...? Seriously? Don't do it!"

The general consensus was that marriage wasn't going to be my thing. I was never a great boyfriend and everyone knew it. Hell, I knew it! I met Monica Diaz on New Year's Eve, 2009. Monica was the best friend of my L.A. assistant's (Eddie's) sister. She was quiet and knew "how to hang." Knowing "how to hang" was important to me. I'd had girlfriends who were jealous, needy and sometimes difficult. They didn't start out that way, but over time, that's how they became. I'm sure if you were to ask them, they'd probably describe me the same way: jealous, needy and sometimes difficult. Being in a relationship with a performer or artist is challenging. We're not normal; we don't work nine to five; and with the greater levels of success, we're used to being indulged. It doesn't make for good partner material. But Monica knew how to hang. She wasn't clingy. She was easy-going and chill. She was just what I needed.

Within three months, Monica and I were together and I told myself that she was the one. In June, while I was on tour in Chicago, Monica sent me a text.

"What time is it over there?" she asked.

"It's midnight," I replied.

The next thing she sent me was a picture of a positive home pregnancy test (you know ... the kind you have to pee on) with the text, "Happy Father's Day! Can't wait to meet you, Daddy!"

"I was ecstatic. I was going to be a father."

I started texting her back but then realized, 'Holy shit, I should probably phone her!" My eyes filled with tears. I was ecstatic. I was going to be a father.

Four weeks later, I asked Monica to marry me. We were at LAX—Los Angeles International Airport—waiting for our bags at the luggage carousel. There were these two baggage handlers who recognized me and asked me when my next show was and then started asking me about my sneakers. As much as I love talking to my fans, there was something that I had to do. However, their conversation did work out to be the perfect distraction for Monica.

We chatted for a second and then, while talking to the guys, I started typing a text to Monica, who was looking for our bags. I sent her an animated emoticon of a guy holding a ring box and then across the screen a message that said, "Will You Marry Me?" Then the emoticon opened the ring box. However, Monica didn't have her phone out. I asked her, "Where's your phone?"

"What's up with you and my phone?" she replied. (I'd been asking her where her phone was since we got off the plane.)

"Check your phone!" I told her.

As she was pulling her phone out of her hand bag, I was fumbling around in my carry-on, looking for the ring box. She opened her phone and said, "Ha Ha." She turned around, looked down and there I was on one knee, with the ring box open in my hand. "Oh my

God! Oh my God!" she started jumping up and down and sweating profusely, and I mean profusely!

"Did that just happen? Was that for real?" the two baggage handlers started asking. And then Monica planted a big, salty, sweaty kiss on me at the luggage carousel at LAX. We were engaged.

On August 20, we got married in Las Vegas. Why Vegas, and why so soon? Vegas, because we didn't want to do a big wedding. It just didn't feel like us. We wanted something low-key and kind of fun, with a few close friends and family . . . and an Elvis impersonator. And that's just what we got. The wedding was great. We had our reception at the Cuban restaurant at the Howard Johnson's next door (pretty classy, huh?). That night, we went back to my house in Henderson and basically hung out with everyone. It was a great day.

"I went from being a middle-aged, self-indulgent bachelor . . . to being a married man with a pregnant wife."

I was a month shy of turning forty and the same age as my father when he got married. Whether I want to admit it or not, both my age and my father's age when he got married were factors in my decision to get married when I did. I was also going to be busy filming a movie and travelling until Christmas, and August was the only time available to me until the following year. Another reason was this: I wanted to be married before my daughter was born—even though all my friends reminded me that I'd grown up with enough West Indians to know that you don't have to be married to have a baby.

All of a sudden, I went from being a middle-aged, self-indulgent bachelor who had never lived with anyone other than his brother, to being a married man with a pregnant wife (whom I'd known for exactly nine months). Over the next four weeks I'd be:

1) Recording my new DVD in London. 2) Starring in and executive producing a movie. 3) Releasing my first book and touring to support the release.

Monica had gone from being a suburban girl from a small town forty miles from Los Angeles where she managed an after-school program for at-risk teens, to being pregnant and living in a mansion in Studio City, and now I was bringing her to London, England, and then to Toronto for a month of filming. We didn't have time to establish what was going to be 'normal' for us and it took its toll. Those early days were challenging, to say the least. I was under a lot of pressure to perform, and Monica was hormonal and a stranger in a strange land. She needed a husband and a stable home, but I couldn't provide those things at that time. We should have been spending those first weeks of marriage getting to know each other better, but I was coming home tired and had to leave her alone at my house in Vaughan, Ontario, for long periods of time because of the movie. Within a matter of days of coming to Toronto, we were fighting and arguing and it was affecting my work on the film. It felt like this wasn't the same girl I'd gotten to know at the beginning of the year, and with all the pressure I was under, I don't know if Monica felt she knew me either. It was also hard to say what was normal since I didn't know what normal was, given the brief time we'd known each other.

Somehow, we made it through those first four months—although they were more difficult than either one of us ever imagined they'd be—and finally found ourselves back home in Los Angeles at the beginning of December, getting things ready for the baby, which was due in late February. We were doing our best to get into some kind of "normal" routine. On December 13, my buddy Michael Bublé was doing a show at the Staples Center in Los Angeles and he hooked us up with tickets for the show. The seats were great and Bublé was fantastic. Honestly, the guy is unbelievably talented and he puts on a great show and he's a great dude.

After the show we went back-stage and saw Michael. It was a zoo. Larry King was back there, and we ended up hanging out with Michael's parents and his fiancée, Luisana. Monica and Luisana had a conversation in Spanish about her and Michael's wedding plans and talked engagement rings and other girl stuff. I was all excited about going to the after-party, but then Monica started to feel nauseous. She started sweating and thought she had food poisoning from the pretzel that I bought her earlier that evening. Monica felt like she was going to pass out, so she lay down on the couch in Michael's dressing room. By this point, everybody had left for the after-party. It was just Monica, me and Michael's assistant, Holly. I had to concede to the fact that I was now not going to the after-party, and I had to admit that I was pretty pissed off about it. We headed back home to Studio City, where I went straight into a deep sleep as soon as I got into bed. (I'd been travelling for twelve hours to get back to L.A. from Detroit, where my flight was cancelled due to a snowstorm. I was exhausted.) However, Monica spent the night puking her guts out. I had assumed that she would feel better after

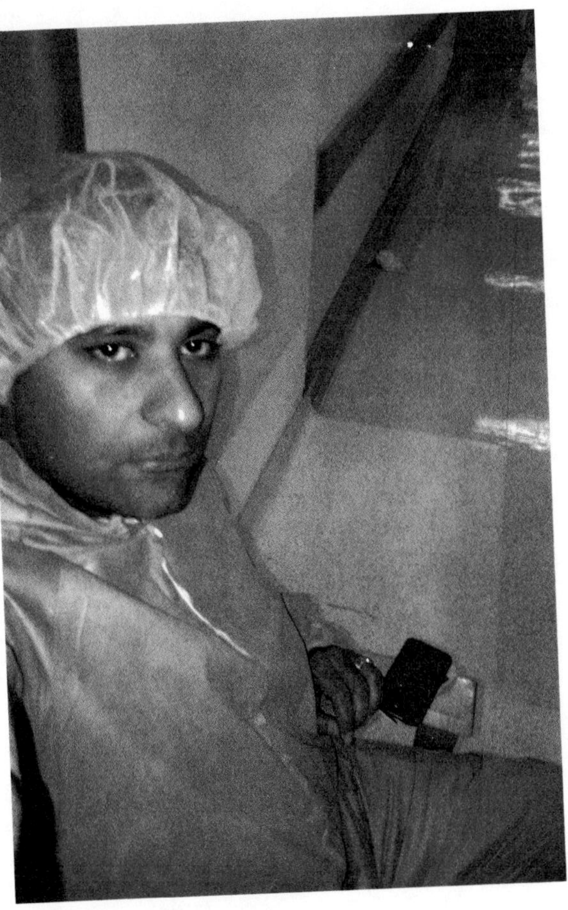

In scrubs, freaking out, waiting for an update on the baby.

vomiting a few times, and continued to sleep. Monica didn't sleep a wink. In the morning I called the on-call doctor at the hospital and she prescribed anti-nausea medication. She did say that if Monica couldn't hold down water that she should come in for an IV to prevent dehydration. By 2:30, nothing was getting better so we decided to head for the hospital.

When we arrived, Monica was put into a wheelchair and we were sent to Labour and Delivery. The nurse took Monica's vitals and called the doctor in right away. Monica's blood pressure was 205, and then all hell broke loose: doctors, nurses, IVs, blood tests and lots of chatter between all the staff. They were going to have to do an emergency C-section, because both the baby and Monica were in danger. As all this was unfolding, I kept leaving the room and going into the bathroom. Once alone, I would break down and cry. I was freaking out. I didn't know what to do or what I was going to do. I texted my brother. I texted Monica's brother, Frank. We'd already called her parents on the way to the hospital, but I didn't want them to panic, so I told Frank to tell them to get to the hospital as soon as possible but not to tell them exactly what was happening. I asked my brother to let my mother know what was happening as well. When I came out of the bathroom, the doctor put me in scrubs. An ultrasound revealed that the baby was very, very small but that they had no choice but to move ahead with the C-section. Monica had developed pre-eclampsia and delivering the baby was the only way to make her blood pressure go down.

Monica was taken into the operating room and then they brought me in. There must have been at least twelve people in the room—five doctors and a bunch of nurses. Monica fell in and out of consciousness after the epidural. I held her hand, kissed her forehead and tried to keep her calm—all while I was completely panicking, crying and trying not to lose it. Within twenty minutes, the medical team had yanked our daughter out of danger and placed her into an incubator. Monica was now safe, but the baby only weighed one pound, ten ounces. The Neonatal Intensive Care Unit team kicked in right away, much like a pit crew at NASCAR. They swarmed the baby and pulled her into consciousness. They brought her over to Monica for a quick kiss and then took her back and went back to work on her. We named the baby Crystianna—after my Mom's middle name of Christina. I thought this would be a nice shout out to Mom. I was wrong. "My name's Christina, not Crystianna," Mom told me. Oh well. We gave her the middle name Marie, after Monica's mom.

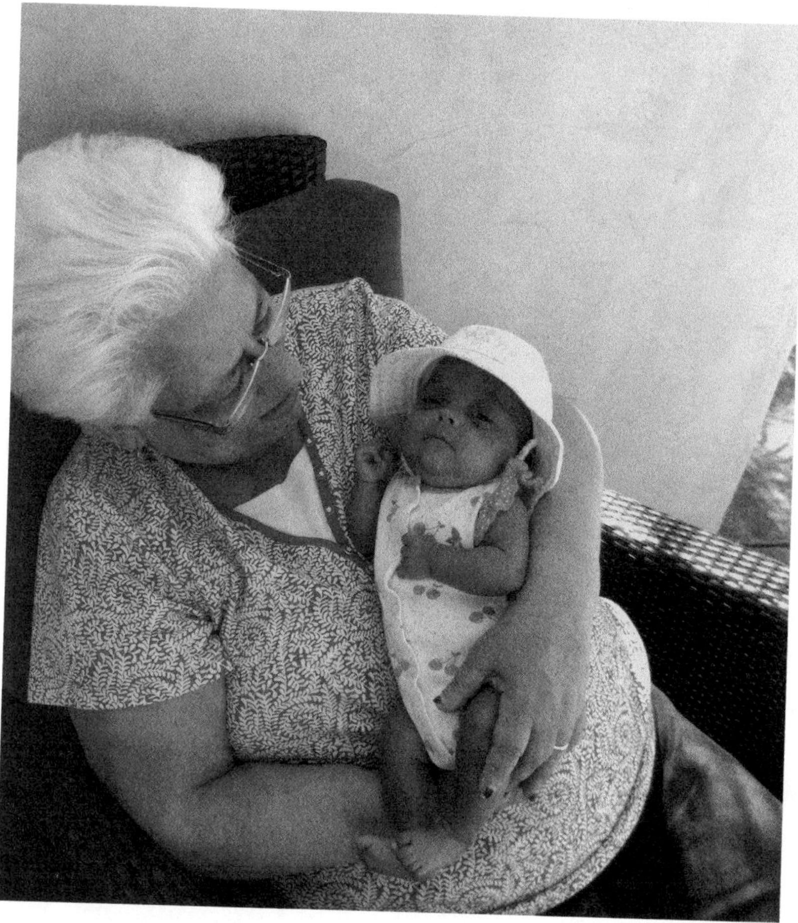

Mama the happy grandmother, with Crystianna.

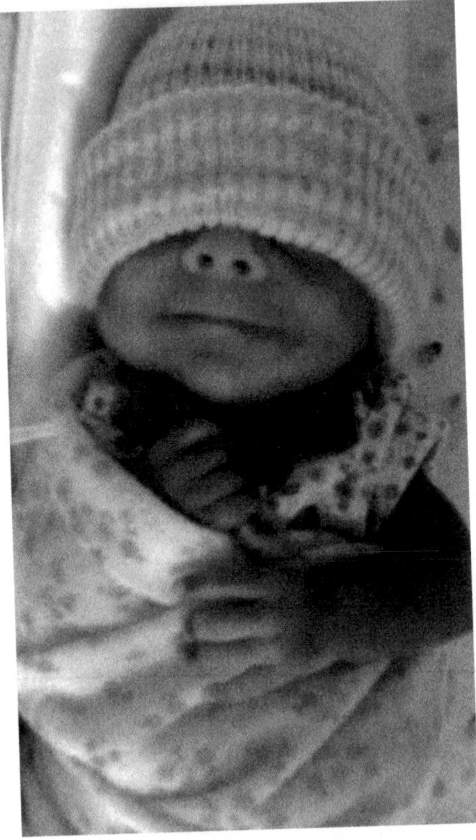

Crystianna Marie Peters, in her first month of life.

Although she was so tiny, Crystianna Marie Peters, was a fighter. She was breathing on her own after two hours. Even the NICU team couldn't believe it. Crystianna remained in the hospital for the next two months. Now here's the thing that really freaked me out when I first saw her: she looked exactly like my dad. It was amazing. Everyone could see it. My dad always wanted a girl and now here she was.

Monica spent every day going back and forth to the hospital and getting as ready as she could for Crystianna to come home. I was out on tour for most of January and the beginning of February and saw my daughter as often as I could between tour dates. On February 22, one day before her actual due date, Crystianna came home. She weighed three pounds, fourteen ounces. Monica and I didn't sleep that first night. Crystianna wasn't really sleeping and we didn't know what to do. We were scared, happy, excited, freaked out, worried ... you name it. I knew my life would never be the same. My love for Crystianna is the most natural

"My dad always wanted a girl and now here she was."

love I've experienced. It's like loving your parents. You don't think about it. It just is. She's Daddy's girl. She smiles when she hears my voice and stares at me like she recognizes me. It's like nothing I've ever felt before and I love it.

ABOUT RUSSELL PETERS

Born in Toronto and raised in Brampton, Ontario, Russell Peters is a global comedy rockstar and internet sensation. His YouTube clips have been viewed over 70 million times and he has performed to sold-out crowds at Toronto's Air Canada Centre, New York's Madison Square Garden, the Sydney Opera House and London's O2 Arena, where he established a new attendance record.

Over the course of his twenty-plus-year career, he has headlined comedy festivals throughout North America and has performed sold-out arena tours of the United States, Canada, India, China, South Africa, Australia, the UK, Singapore, Sweden, Norway, the United Arab Emirates, Beirut, Jordan, Bahrain and the Philippines. Peters has appeared on Showtime, Comedy Central, HBO, the CBC, BBC, CTV, CNN, TBS, CBS, ABC and NBC. In 2009 and 2010 he was listed on the *Forbes* list of top-earning comedians in the United States, along with Chris Rock and Jerry Seinfeld.

ABOUT THE CO-AUTHORS

CLAYTON PETERS is Russell's brother and manager. He lives in Oakville, Ontario with his wife Emma and their dog, Zoe. He commutes between Russell's live dates globally and Los Angeles, and oversees all aspects of his brother's career.

DANNIS KOROMILAS is an acclaimed screenwriter and co-creator/producer of the police drama *The Bridge*. He is presently developing the Cold War television series *REVOLUTION '68*. He lives in Toronto with his wife and two sons.